101 Amazing
WOMEN

Extraordinary Heroines
Throughout History

Jack Goldstein

101 Amazing Women
Published in 2016 by
Acorn Books
www.acornbooks.co.uk

Typography and layout by
Andrews UK Limited
www.andrewsuk.com

Copyright © 2016 Jack Goldstein

The right of Jack Goldstein Higgins to be identified as author of this book has been asserted in accordance with section 77 and 78 of the Copyrights Designs and Patents Act 1988.

This book is sold subject to the condition that it shall not, by way of trade or otherwise, be lent, resold, hired out or otherwise circulated without the publisher's prior written consent in any form of binding or cover other than that in which it is published, and without a similar condition being imposed on the subsequent purchaser.

All facts contained within this book have been researched from reputable sources. If any information is found to be false, please contact the publishers, who will be happy to make corrections for future editions.

The values and opinions expressed herein belong to the author and/or researchers and do not necessarily reflect those of Acorn Books or Andrews UK Limited.

Photograph Credits:
Template of Hatshepsut courtesy of *Olaf Tausch*
Hanna Reitsch courtesy of *Archiv der Gerhard-Fieseler-Stiftung*
Angela Merkel courtesy of *Dirk Vorderstraße*

Contents

Earlier History. 1

Transport. 11

Politics 27

Human Rights. 39

Warfare. 51

Girls & Young Women 69

Sport 83

Literature. 95

Science & Technology 107

Business 123

Media & Entertainment 130

And Finally... 136

To my mother, an amazing woman

Introduction

There are so many women who have contributed to the development of our society that the hardest thing about writing a book such as this is simply deciding who will and will not be featured in it. I make no claim whatsoever as to whether those I have included are more important or deserving in any way than those who I have not – I have simply tried my best to give the reader a light introduction to the background of individuals from a range of periods, countries and areas of interest.

The full story of every single one of the women featured in this book is undoubtedly fascinating and I am sure that somewhere on the internet or at your local library, you will find a great deal more information on any one of them than I have supplied.

My greatest – and humblest – hope for this book is simply to inspire both women and men to continue the work started by others whose stories I tell within these pages. If you read them and are entertained, inspired or even just simply relieved of boredom, then you'll have made me very happy.

Jack Goldstein
September 2016

101 Amazing Women

Chapter One
Earlier History

Hatshepsut
(1507–1458 BC)

The fifth pharaoh of ancient Egypt's eighteenth dynasty, Hatshepsut was (we believe) only the second ever female pharaoh, and the one who ruled for the longest – some twenty years. According to many historians, she is the first 'great woman' in history of whom we have knowledge. During her reign, Hatshepsut re-established disrupted trade networks and set up new ones, increasing the dynasty's economic power. She commissioned hundreds of construction projects which were significantly grander than those of her predecessors – some of which were so impressive, later pharaohs tried to claim them as their own! Compared to other leaders, she held a relatively peaceful rule, with expansion coming from trade and diplomacy rather than through battle and conquest. When Hatshepsut died, her step-son, Thutmose III (for whom she had acted as regent) did all he could to eradicate her from history in an effort to assert his own authority, ensuring no-one challenged *his* son for the throne.

Hatshepsut's Temple at Deir el-Bahari

Sappho

(circa 620–570 BC)

Sappho was a poet from the Greek island of Lesbos. We know little about her life, and most of her poetry (of which we believe she wrote around ten thousand lines) is now lost with only fragments surviving. Her works were written to be set to song, and it is the evocative and sensual language she used in them which has ensured her legacy lasts to this very day, even if the majority of her writings don't. In addition to writing about (and paying homage to) the deities of her time, Sappho's poems expressed love for both women and men. There is some debate as to whether the poems were intended to be performed in public or alternatively in a more private, personal setting. Even as recently as 2013, parts of her work have continued to be rediscovered, some not without controversy; the exact circumstances of the most recent unearthing is questionable, shrouded under a veil of secrecy.

Anyte of Tegea

(circa 3rd century BC)

More complete poems by Anyte of Tegea have survived to this day than by any other ancient Greek female writer. Listed by Antipater of Thessalonica as one of the nine early muses, Anyte was the leader of a school of poetry and literature in the southern Greek region of Peloponnese, which included the famous lyric poet Leonidas of Tarentum. She is thought to be the first poet ever to have written epitaphs for animals and is certainly one of the first to write vivid descriptions of untamed nature. Known as 'the female Homer' she was so highly thought of in ancient times that hers were the very first poems listed in a collection of epigrams by some fifty different writers of the period. Although we know very little about her life, her poetry seems to focus on the world around her, rather than on more common but intangible concepts such love and feelings.

Cleopatra

(69–30 BC)

The last active Ptolemaic pharaoh, Cleopatra solidified her grip on the Egyptian throne first by having a son with Julius Caesar, and later through her relationship with Roman leader Mark Anthony. Using her beauty and charm to great political advantage, Cleopatra was also renowned for her intellect; amazingly, she spoke at least *nine* languages and rarely required an interpreter. Famously she is said to have committed suicide by inducing an asp (an *Egyptian cobra*) to bite her breast – although most modern historians doubt this story, with suicide by poisoning or even murder being proposed as alternatives.

Boudica

(30–60 AD)

Boudica (sometimes written as *Boudicca*, *Boudicea* and a whole host of other spellings) was queen of the British Celtic *Iceni* tribe. In 60 AD she gathered together her troops, along with those of the *Trinovantes* and other Celtic tribes, and revolted against Roman rule in Britain. She successfully destroyed *Camulodunum* (today known as Colchester) where a temple had been built to the former emperor Claudius. When the Romans heard that her next target was *Londinium* (London), they evacuated the city, and Boudica and her 100,000 tribespeople lay waste to the city, burning it – and later *Verulamium* (St Albans) – to the ground. Her troops killed more than fifty thousand Roman soldiers, and *almost* convinced Emperor Nero to withdraw all Roman troops from Britain. In the end, the Romans re-grouped in the West Midlands, eventually defeating Boudica. According to legend, Boudica took her own life to avoid capture, and in doing so perhaps even added to her fame as one of Britain's most well-known female leaders.

Sarah Bernhardt as Cleopatra in 1891

Lady Trieu
(225–248)

Lady Trieu (for a time) successfully resisted Chinese expansion into her home country of Vietnam. Often referred to as 'the Vietnamese Joan of Arc', Trieu is believed to have been orphaned as a young girl. Deciding to forego the traditional Vietnamese female role of staying at home to look after the housework, at the age of twenty she ventured into the mountains, gathering together a band of a thousand followers. For six months, Trieu and her warriors fought back against the advancing Chinese; she was known to join battle wearing yellow robes, riding on the back of an elephant! Sadly, the invasion was a war of attrition, and the Chinese simply had more forces available to fight and die even though Trieu's band were the more skilful. Lady Trieu is quoted as saying, *"I'd like to ride storms, kill sharks in the open sea, drive out the aggressors, reconquer the country, undo the ties of serfdom, and never bend my back to be the concubine of whatever man."*

Empress Theodora
(500–548)

As the wife of Justinian I, Theodora was empress of the Byzantine Empire. Whilst her husband held *official* power, many scholars have proposed that she was the *real* decision-maker, with Justinian essentially a 'co-regent'. Theodora achieved many great feats during her time in power, with the suppression of the *Nika revolt* (a devastating riot that threatened the empire's entire political system) being one of the most lauded. She is credited with a range of social reforms, mostly involving the rights of women. These included expanding the rights of women in both property ownership and divorce proceedings, giving mothers guardianship rights over their children, forbidding the killing of women for adultery and even closing brothels, creating instead convents where the former prostitutes could live in safety.

The mosaic 'Empress Theodora and Her Court' from the Basilica of San Vitale in Ravenna

WU ZETIAN

(624–705)

Originally concubine to one emperor (Taizong), Wu Zetian married his successor, Emperor Gaozong, becoming his empress consort. When Gaozong suffered a stroke thus becoming unable to perform his courtly duties, Wu Zetian became administrator of the court, effectively giving her the *power* of the emperor if not the *title*. Under her guidance, the Chinese expire extended further than ever before whilst improving education and the fate of the ordinary citizen. Even in a heavily male-dominated court, Wu's strength, determination and careful rule saw her subjects enjoy a golden age of knowledge and expansion.

ELIZABETH I

(1533–1603)

On the 9th of August 1588, Queen Elizabeth I addressed her troops at Tilbury. There, she famously said *"I know I have the body of a weak, feeble woman; but I have the heart and stomach of a king, and of a king of England too"*. Her father, Henry VIII, had been a strong leader, but following his reign there had been a power struggle between his children; it was to be one of the most important in English history as it eventually established England as a *Protestant* rather than *Catholic* nation. Throughout her reign, Elizabeth proved herself to be a powerful and decisive leader, and until Queen Victoria hundreds of years later remained the country's most influential female figure. Under Elizabeth's reign, culture flourished and what we now refer to as *the Elizabethan era* saw English drama flourish, notably of course through the works of William Shakespeare – although he was certainly not alone in this regard. It was also during this period that England's seafaring prowess increased more so than ever before, seeing adventurers

Elizabeth I of England

such as Sir Francis Drake explore areas of the world previously unknown to the Western world. Elizabeth never took a husband, and is quoted as declaring herself married to England and her subjects.

CHING SHIH
(1775–1844)

In the early 19th century, Ching Shih (also known to some as *Cheng I Sao*) terrorised the China Sea. The leading pirate of her day, she directly commanded a significant personal navy: some three hundred ships with a crew of around thirty thousand sailors and had significant influence over an even larger fleet of fifteen hundred vessels (crewed by 180,000 seafaring men, women and children). Every empire of the time feared this *'widow of Zheng'* (as her name translates into English) with her fleet entering into conflict against the Qing Dynasty, the British, the Portuguese and many other world powers. Ching married into a successful pirate family, and when her husband Cheng I died, she used his connections and her political nous to negotiate her way into a position of incredible power. She issued her own pirate code (which was fair, strict and *always* enforced) which included the group inspection of booty and the investment of 'profits' in the fleet, ensuring damaged ships were re-supplied and repaired well in time for their next encounter. Shih remains one of the few pirates in history to have ever successfully retired from her life of crime, which she did in 1810 when the Chinese government offered her an amnesty – even agreeing that she could keep her ill-gotten gains! Ching Shih didn't much fancy a quiet retirement however, and decided to open a gambling house which she ran for the rest of her life.

Chapter Two
Transport

Grace Darling
(1815–1842)

Grace Darling was the daughter of a lighthouse keeper in Northumberland, England. On the night of the 6th September 1838, a ship called the *Forfarshire* ran aground on rocks near to her family's lighthouse; when looking out a window in the early hours of the 7th September, Grace could see the wreck of the ship (which by then had broken apart) and the survivors, who were stranded on a low, rocky outcrop known as Big Harcar. She alerted her father, and the two decided that it was far too rough weather for a lifeboat to be put out from the nearest rescue station; they therefore launched to sea themselves in a four-man rowing boat and heroically rowed the mile-long journey to the outcrop, all the while battling against terrible storms and high waves. A number of survivors were rescued, and were rowed back to the lighthouse. Grace Darling's attentiveness and heroism that night saved the lives of both men and women, and she was awarded the silver medal of bravery by the organisation that would go on to become the *Royal National Lifeboat Association*. The whole country was told of her rescue attempt, and £700 in reward money was raised for her – including £50 given by Queen Victoria herself! Sadly, Grace fell ill just a few years later and died of tuberculosis at the age of 26. Darling is not forgotten by the residents of Northumberland however; a cenotaph recognises her bravery in a local churchyard, and a modern-day RNLI lifeboat based at Seahouses is named after her.

Mary Anderson
(1866–1953)

Some inventions are so simple yet brilliant, we hardly notice them and rarely give them a second thought – but without them it would be nearly impossible to live life as we do today. When it comes to

Grace Darling

transportation, the windscreen wiper is surely one of these such technologies. Almost every vehicle in the world has a set – from cars to planes, ships to giant diggers and everything in between – ensuring that even in the heaviest rain, the driver or operator can still safely command their machines. Yet before 1903, no such thing existed. Even by then, cars could travel at a speed whereby rain, sleet and snow could cause serious visibility problems, but no-one had been able to properly address the problem. In an industry at that point dominated by men, it therefore may be surprising to learn that in that year, a patent was granted to Mary Anderson for an automatic car window cleaning device she called the *windshield wiper*. Anderson had been visiting New York City on a particularly cold day, and noticed that despite the temperature, the driver had both panes of the front window fully opened – it seemed preferable to be bitterly cold but still be able to see the road than the alternative! On her return to her native Alabama, Mary worked with a designer and local engineering company to produce a working model of an idea she had had – a lever that would be situated inside the vehicle connected via a spring-loaded arm to a rubber blade on the outside. With a counterweight ensuring contact between wiper and window, the lever could make the blade move back and forth across the window, thus clearing it of any unwanted residue. Although the idea *had* been tried before, Mary Anderson was the first person able to make an *effective* version. Having perfected her design, in 1905 Anderson attempted to sell the device to a Canadian firm, but they felt there was no commercial value in such as invention. Yet after 1920 – when the patent had expired – car manufacturing rates increased, and the car companies began to add wipers using Mary Anderson's design. Within two years they had become extremely popular, and Cadillac became the first company to adopt them as standard equipment – with most other companies following soon after.

Baroness Raymonde de Laroche of France

(1882–1919)

As a youngster, anything and everything mechanical interested Elise Raymonde Deroche. She loved to watch automobiles being driven and worked on (at the time they were still a relatively new invention) and was also a fan of motorcycles. However, it was Wilbur Wright's 1908 visit to Paris which *really* inspired Raymonde (as she used as a stage name for her acting career). That year he demonstrated his new flying machine to the French public, and many were utterly captivated by this astonishing sight. Deroche happened to be acquainted with a number of people who moved in the exclusive aviation circle, and she vowed to take up flying herself. One close friend was aeroplane builder Charles Voisin; Raymonde begged him to teach her how to fly. This he did – although not without difficulty… his plane could only seat one person, so she had to operate the controls in the air whilst he stood on the ground shouting instructions! After some taxiing, she took off and flew around three hundred yards, marking the first time a woman had been a pilot for a powered flight. Although she was denied the opportunity to fly during the First World War (the 'top brass' considered it too dangerous a job for a woman) she did continue her flying career in peacetime, setting two women's altitude records and the women's distance flying record in 1919. Later that year however, de Laroche was involved in the crash of an experimental aircraft that she was co-piloting (and that she had worked on as an engineer) which tragically killed both her and her co-pilot.

Raymonde de Laroche

Olive Dennis
(1885–1957)

In 1920 Olive Dennis became only the second ever woman to obtain a degree in Civil Engineering from Cornell University. After graduating, she was hired by the B&O Railroad to work in their bridges department, where she worked on the design of a number of structures. She was later promoted to the role of Service Engineer (and is considered by some to be the first ever person to have held such a position anywhere in America). It was in this role that Dennis truly changed the entire experience of rail travel. For many years, standard rail carriages had been functional but not necessarily comfortable or enjoyable in which to ride. All this changed with Olive's numerous introductions that included reclining seats, dressing rooms of increased size with free soap, paper towels and drinking cups, dimmable lights, a patented individual window vent system, stain-resistant upholstery and later even air-conditioned carriages. In fact, the upgrades to the passenger rail system that were made by Olive Dennis caused huge numbers of passengers to choose rail travel over road, and both the buses and airlines had to conduct a similar overhaul of *their* passenger services to attract travellers back to their respective modes of transport! Olive rightly believed that many businesses would do well to gain a woman's point of view, and is quoted as saying *"No matter how successful a business may seem to be, it can gain even greater success if it gives consideration to the woman's viewpoint."*

Bessie Coleman
(1892–1926)

Bessie Coleman's father was part Cherokee, and her mother an African American. This meant that she – being of mixed race – was not afforded the same opportunities as white girls of her age at the time. Educated in a segregated school, she nonetheless proved herself to be an intelligent student, and rather than continue to work in the cotton farms she had helped her father harvest as a schoolgirl, she chose to move to Chicago and found employment as a manicurist in a barber's shop. There she heard the fantastic tales of pilots who had returned from the First World War, and decided that she herself was going to become a pilot. With American segregation at the time, her dream proved difficult to achieve; no flying school would train either women or black people of any gender. Yet with financial assistance from a generous backer, she took classes to become fluent in French and in 1920 travelled to Paris to earn her pilot's license, which she was successfully awarded on the 15th of June 1921. She therefore became both the first female pilot of African American descent *and* the first female pilot of Native American descent! On her return to America Bessie became a media sensation, and took to performing barnstorming stunts in front of paying audiences. For years she was a huge draw, and broke through the racial barrier to be respected by people of all colours. In 1926, she needed to replace her existing plane, and bought a second-hand Curtiss Jenny. It turned out to have been poorly maintained however, and after being forced to make three emergency landings in just one trip from Florida to Dallas, her family implored her not to continue to fly in it. Coleman ignored their advice though, and on the 30th April that year she took it out for a flight to explore some local terrain. Planning a parachute jump for the next day, she didn't put on her seatbelt as she wanted to be able to stand up and look over the cockpit sill for a better view. Ten minutes into the flight, the plane fell into an uncontrolled spin, and Bessie tragically fell to her death from a height of over six hundred metres. Memorials to this pioneering aviator can be found across America, and a road at Chicago's world famous O'Hare airport is named after her.

Bessie Coleman

Amelia Earhart
(1897–1937?)

In 1920, at the age of 23, Amelia Earhart took a short plane ride that changed her life; she knew straight afterwards that she was 'meant' to fly. Earhart worked hard to earn the thousand dollars which paid for enough flying lessons for her to be able to fly solo. On the 21st of May 1932, Amelia established a new record time for solo flight across the Atlantic: 13.5 hours. Five years later Earhart, along with navigator Fred Noonan, set out to fly around the world. But at 8:45pm on the 2nd of July 1937, the pair sent a frantic message to the US Coast Guard. Having left New Guinea for Howland Island, the two were never seen again. As wreckage of the plane was never found, some conspiracy theories exist suggesting the two may have planned the disappearance and run off together – although most historians feel this is rather unlikely, the truth being a devastating crash which tragically ended their lives.

Mariette Hélène Delangle
(1900–1984)

At the age of sixteen, Mariette Hélène Delangle travelled the 47 miles from her village home to Paris where she found work in the city's music halls. She chose to use the stage name *Hélène Nice*, which over time became *Hellé Nice*. She was absolutely loved by the patrons, especially when she partnered with a man named Robert Lisset with whom she ended up performing in the best clubs across the whole of Europe. With income from both performing and modelling projects she undertook, Hellé found herself with more money than she had ever dreamed of. She bought her own home and even a yacht, but her true love was fast cars – especially after she damaged her knee in a skiing accident, which ended her dancing career. In 1929 Nice began to make a

Amelia Earhart

name for herself in the auto racing world, and through her friend and lover Phillipe de Rothschild she was introduced to Ettore Bugatti, who not only recognised her ability to generate publicity, but also her racing prowess. Bugatti therefore invited Hélène to join his Grand Prix team, which she did, competing in five major Grand Prix races in 1931. Although she did not *win* any of these five races, she certainly gave the top drivers a run for their money, and finished in strong positions each time. Over the next decade or so, Hélène competed in a huge range of auto sport events, from the Monte Carlo Rally and the 1933 Italian Grand Prix to the Mille Miglia and various hill climbs. A serious crash in the 1936 Brazilian Grand Prix almost killed her, but she awoke from a three-day coma and became a national hero in Brazil. Sadly, Nice was accused of being a Nazi collaborator during the Second World War, and became unemployable after hostilities ended. She saw out her old age in poverty in a run-down apartment in the French city that shares her stage name: Nice.

Elinor Smith

(1911–2010)

When she was just sixteen, Elinor Smith became the youngest licensed pilot in the world. Her career saw her rise to the position of test pilot for both aircraft manufacturers Fairchild and Bellanca. Affectionately known to the public as the 'Flying Flapper of Freeport', she was famous for her stunts, one of which saw her fly a biplane under all four of New York's East River bridges. Although the stunt was illegal, the city's mayor only gave her the light punishment of being 'grounded' for ten days – obviously he was as impressed as everyone else! Smith achieved many records during her career as a pilot, including setting the woman's world speed record (190.8 miles per hour) and setting the first official women's record for an endurance flight which included mid-air refuelling. In 1930 she flew a whole mile higher than the previous world altitude record, and impressed media executives so much in the post-flight interview that she became the 'voice' of aviation broadcasting – this still all before her 19th birthday. During the great depression Smith performed aircraft stunts in order to raise money for the poor and the homeless. Over sixty years later she became the oldest pilot to succeed in a simulated space shuttle landing, and at the age of 89 she flew an experimental plane at Langley Air Force Base.

Elinor Smith (right) with Helen Hicks

Hanna Reitsch
(1912–1979)

Hanna Reitsch was the only woman to win the *Iron Cross First Class* and the *Luftwaffe Pilot Badge in Gold with Diamonds* during the Second World War. Both prior to the war and afterwards, she set more than forty women's endurance records including time, distance and altitude flights and as a result is considered Germany's most famous female aviator. Hitler awarded Reitsch the Iron Cross for her work as a test pilot in the Third Reich, in which she was a test pilot for the Junkers Ju 87 dive bomber (often known as a *stuka*) and the Dornier Do 17 (known by some as the 'flying pencil'). In addition to her efforts in winged aircraft, she also holds the honour of being the first ever female helicopter pilot – in fact she conducted *indoor* demonstrations of the Nazi's helicopter technology, and was very much a mainstay of Nazi propaganda. Reitsch even flight-tested the Messerschmitt Me 163 rocket-propelled plane, although one landing went wrong and she spent five months in hospital recovering from the resulting crash. She was committed to her country, and even proposed 'Operation Suicide' to Hitler – essentially a kamikaze gilder bomb, for which seventy men did actually volunteer; although Hitler had doubts (mainly that the war situation was not sufficiently serious to warrant the sacrifice) he approved the project! It was never implemented however, as when the hardware was ready, the Führer felt the suitable window of opportunity had been missed. After the war, Hanna Reitsch set up a gliding school in Ghana. Whilst many who collaborated with the Nazis were punished after the war, it was decided that although she was patriotic, Hanna was simply politically naïve, and did not necessarily support the extreme views held by the senior members of the third Reich.

Hanna Reitsch with Erich Bachem

Ellen MacArthur
(1976–)

On the 7th of February 2005, Ellen MacArthur completed her solo voyage around the world, breaking the world record for the fastest ever solo circumnavigation of the globe by sail. By that point she had been sailing for many years – as a schoolgirl Ellen had put aside much of her school dinner money for three whole years to buy her first boat! This boat was an eight-foot dinghy called *Threp'ny Bit*, and Ellen even taped a real threepenny bit (an old English coin) to its bow. She bought her second boat in 1995 (a Corribee named *Iduna*) which she used to conduct a circumnavigation of Great Britain. Moving onto ever more advanced vessels, she continued to gain recognition in the sailing world, and in 2001 came second in a round-the-world race in a yacht of her own design. Her record solo voyage started on the 28th of November 2004, meaning that it took her 71 days… and fourteen hours, eighteen minutes and thirty-three seconds to be precise – over one day quicker than the previous record holder. In recognition of her incredible voyage, at the age of just 28, MacArthur was made a *Dame Commander of the British Empire*, becoming the youngest ever person to have received such an award. After retiring from professional sailing in 2010, she set up *The Ellen MacArthur Foundation*, a charity that aims to eliminate waste and pollution from the industrial economy.

Chapter Three
Politics

Catherine the Great
(1729–1796)

Catherine II was Russia's longest-ruling empress, with her reign lasting from 1762 until her death thirty-four years later. She oversaw a period of massive expansion in Russian history, with the empire's growth coming from both diplomacy and conquest. It was under Catherine the Great's rule that Russia colonised Alaska – then a Russian territory, but later (in 1867) sold to the USA for just over seven million dollars. Catherine's time in power was a difficult one for many Russian subjects, as her rule relied on *serfdom*; many of those at the bottom of the pyramid were unsurprisingly unhappy with their lot, which led to a number of rebellions – the most famous being *Pugachev's Rebellion* of Cossacks and peasants. Despite this underlying dissatisfaction, Catherine's rule is considered to be the golden age of the Russian Empire, with the construction of many beautiful mansions for the nobility adding to a sense of prosperity. She oversaw a period of enlightenment of her empire, with huge investment in the arts and the setting up of *the Smolny Institute,* Europe's first ever state-financed higher educational establishment for women. Despite rumours to the contrary, Catherine passed away after she had fallen into a coma following a stroke.

Jeanette Rankin
(1880–1973)

In 1916, Jeanette Rankin was elected by the State of Montana to the US House of Representatives, becoming the first ever woman in American history to hold such a position. Twenty-four years later she won a *second* term in the same position. This meant that she was in office for the outbreak of *both* world wars. One of Rankin's greatest causes was civil rights, and in fact she voted against the US joining both wars – of course, she was on the losing side of the

Jeanette Rankin (right)

two votes. When asked in later life about the 1917 ballot, she said *"I felt the first time the first woman had a chance to say no to war, she should say it"*. Rankin also championed gender equality issues, particularly in ensuring women had a vote in all American states, resulting in the Nineteenth Amendment. Her vote for the original resolution ensured she holds an interesting accolade – the only woman in the history of America who voted to give women the right to vote!

Golda Meir
(1898–1978)

In 1969 Golda Meir became Israel's fourth Prime Minister, the only woman ever to have held the office. As a youngster, Meir's family had moved to America after experiencing violence against Jews in the 1905 Kiev pogrom. In her late teenage years, Meir joined a political group which supported the establishment of a Jewish homeland. In 1921 she joined the *Merhavia* kibbutz in Palestine with her husband Morris and three years later moved to Jerusalem. During the Second World War and in light of the Nazi's persecution of the Jewish people she became highly vocal regarding the need for a *full* Jewish state (as opposed to alternative suggestions for only a homeland). When she (and many others) got her wish and Israel declared its independence, Golda Meir was one of the signatories of the declaration. The work Meir undertook for Israel included a secret mission where she went undercover (in fact disguised as an Arab) to plead with King Abdullah of Jordan not to enter into a war with her country (a plea which he declined). Although she was ready to retire at the age of 68, Meir served the remaining term of Prime Minister Eshkol after his death, and then won a four-year term in the next election. During her time in power, Meir took military and economic aid from President Nixon, a move which allowed her to negotiate peace talks with the Arab nations from a position of strength. Towards the end of her tenure, hostilities broke out in what is now referred to as the *Yom Kippur War*. After three weeks of fighting, Israel was victorious – in fact gaining territory. By now however Meir had served her country for many years longer than she had intended, and was exhausted. She resigned from office but remained an important political figure until her death from leukaemia at the age of 1978.

Golda Meir

Indira Gandhi in 1966

Indira Gandhi
(1917–1984)

India's first female prime minister, Indira Gandhi held the position for three consecutive terms from 1966 to 1977, and a fourth from 1980 until 1984, when she was assassinated by her own bodyguards. Gandhi was known for her strong political stance, often taking ruthless (but generally seen as necessary) decisions in her career. She led India to war with Pakistan over the issue of independence for Bangladesh, at the same time developing India's economy into the strongest in South Asia, arguably turning the country into a significant world power. In one BBC poll, Indira Gandhi was voted the greatest woman of the past thousand years!

Margaret Thatcher
(1925–2013)

The 1980s saw huge change in the UK. Traditional industries such as mining were closed forever, leading to millions of people becoming unemployed. Yet at the same time, the country's economy was growing like never before. At the forefront of this change was Margaret Thatcher, often referred to as 'Maggie'. Few elements of her time in power are without their controversy. The introduction of the poll tax saw unprecedented riots across the country; the Falklands War saw most of the country unite in a wave of patriotism – but questions were asked about the sinking of the Belgrano which some claimed was returning to port. The sector of the population that most vocally stood against Thatcher were the country's poorer communities, yet arguably she helped them more than any other modern politician had ever done by giving them the opportunity to buy their council houses under the 'right to buy' scheme, which saw the UK change from a nation of renters to one of home-owners. Hated and loved in equal measure, she proved that a woman could be just as strong and controversial a figure in politics as any man!

Jóhanna Sigurðardóttir
(1942–)

In 2009 at the peak of a long political career, Joanna Sigurðardóttir was elected Prime Minister of Iceland. In doing so, she became the world's first ever openly lesbian head of government. When she retired in 2012, Jóhanna was the country's longest-serving Member of Parliament, having been first elected back in 1978. The next year she became deputy speaker, and continued to hold important positions throughout her career, including Minister for Social affairs in four different cabinets. As Prime Minister, she oversaw an extremely difficult period in Iceland's history – the financial crisis which had crippled the world – which even included a change to the country's constitution that had been in place for over one hundred years. In 2010, Sigurðardóttir's government became the first Western one to ban strip clubs and any other form of employment which saw employer's profit from employees' nudity. In doing so, some claimed that Iceland had in a single stroke become the most feminist country in the world.

Aung San Suu Kyi
(1945–)

In 1988, Suu Kyi formed the National League for Democracy in her home country of Myanmar (formerly Burma), with a view to bringing democratic rule there. Despite being put under house arrest by the government for most of the time since, she has worked tirelessly to bring about change. She was released from house arrest in 2010, and in 2012 her party finally won a huge majority in the country's first democratic elections. Suu Kyi is generally recognised across the Western world as one of the most influential and dedicated proponents of democracy in a troubled region and amongst many other awards was given the 1991 Nobel Prize for Peace.

Aung San Suu Kyi

Angela Merkel

Benazir Bhutto
(1953–2007)

Bhutto served as the prime minister of Pakistan twice, the first time from 1988 until 1990 and the second from 1993 to 1996. When she was elected in 1988, Bhutto became the first woman in history to have been democratically chosen as the leader of a nation with an Islamic majority electorate. During her time as leader of Pakistan, she helped the country develop into a modern nation; her focus on industrial growth and development and financial deregulation saw Pakistan emerge as a true player on the world stage. Her tough stance saw comparisons with Margaret Thatcher (the two were in charge of their respective nations at the same time) and both were referred to by their country's media as *'the Iron Lady'*. Although Bhutto went into exile in Dubai after her party was ousted in 1996 amongst claims of corruption, she returned to her country in 2007. She quickly became the favourite candidate to win the next general election but was assassinated at one of her political party's campaign rallies by a bomb that was set off near to the vehicle in which she was standing.

Angela Merkel
(1954–)

In 2005, Angela Merkel was elected Chancellor of Germany, the world's fourth largest economy. Merkel has been a politician since the fall of the Berlin Wall, when she was a deputy spokesperson for the very first democratically-elected East German government. In terms of Europe, Merkel was the key player in negotiating the Treaty of Lisbon (which modernised the constitution of the EU) and ensured the EU's relatively smooth recovery from the financial crisis which shook the world in the mid-to-late 2000s. She successfully kept the EU working together as a political unit (with the exception of the UK who voted to leave the organisation) even through tough times including multiple financial bail-outs to Greece. Even though it has not been a popular stance amongst all Germans, she has seen her country take in an extraordinary number of refugees (mainly from Africa and the Middle East) and give them a new start. Widely respected for her political success and influence, Angela Merkel has been named the most powerful woman in the world in ten separate years by *Forbes* Magazine.

Condoleezza Rice
(1954–)

In 2005 Condoleezza Rice became America's first ever female African-American Secretary of State. Prior to holding this highly respected position, Rice had been professor of political science at Stanford University and was well-known for her incisive strategic thinking. She pioneered a policy known as *Transformational Diplomacy*, which focused on increasing the number of democratic governments in the world, particularly in the Middle East. She up-skilled American diplomats in locations such as Iraq and Afghanistan, ensuring not only that they had a deeper understanding of the issues relevant to their respective regions, but also that they became fluent in *two* foreign languages to improve communication and trust. Whilst many considered her president's stance to be one of aggression, Rice brought an air of compassion and diplomacy to the table.

Chapter Four
Human Rights

Mary Wollstonecraft
(1759–1979)

In 1792, Mary wrote *A Vindication of the Rights of Woman*, a hugely important book in the early feminist movement. In this, she laid out a clearly-presented argument showing that women were not naturally inferior to men, only seeming to appear so due to lack of education. She is today considered to be one of the founding feminist philosophers. For many years, Mary was not given the respect afforded to her in the modern age; when she died, her husband published a memoir of her life which detailed what others at the time saw as rather immoral lifestyle choices. For almost one hundred years this destroyed her reputation, meaning her writings were not given due consideration. It was with the birth of the feminist movement of the late 19th century that views on the ethics of her affairs were rightly ignored and thus her philosophy began to garner the respect it deserved. Mary sadly died from childbirth; she passed away eleven years after giving birth to a daughter named Mary – a writer we know today as Mary Shelley.

Margaret Fuller
(1810–1850)

Margaret Fuller was an advocate not only for women's rights, but also for reform in the penal system and the emancipation of slaves. She is best remembered for her book *Woman in the Nineteenth Century*, which is considered to be the first major American feminist work. In her thirties, Margaret had a reputation for being extremely well-read (some said the best in New England at the time) and she was the first woman given access to the library at Harvard. Despite some of her contemporaries describing her as a 'talker rather than an activist', many later feminists cite Fuller as a source of their inspiration. After her death, she was somewhat forgotten for many years; editors believed her fame would be short-lived and even altered much of her writing before publication. As with other early feminist figures, it has only been in relatively recent times that Fuller's writing and philosophy has been revisited and recognised as a hugely important step in the fight for women's rights.

Margaret Fuller

Emmeline Pankhurst

Emmeline Pankhurst
(1858–1928)

At the turn of the 20th Century, women in England were effectively treated as second-class citizens. Importantly, they did not have the right to vote in national elections. Emmeline, as head of the *Women's Social and Political Union*, campaigned against this inequality and injustice, with the group often using what could today be considered terrorist tactics to get their point across – bombs and arson were controversially amongst the methods used by members of the group. In the end, Emmeline's campaign was successful, and just two weeks before her death in June 1928, an act establishing voting equality for men and women was passed. Whether the end justifies the means is a question that is far too difficult to discuss in a book such as this, however Pankhurst certainly felt her groups' actions were necessary, and they undoubtedly achieved a huge step forward in terms of women's rights.

Helen Keller
(1880–1968)

When she was just nineteen months old, Helen Keller suffered a severe illness which left her both deaf and blind. She experienced a difficult childhood, but when she reached the age of seven, she learned how to overcome her disabilities through her friendship with a teacher, Anne Sullivan. Anne initially taught Helen using hand-touching signals, and over time she became proficient in Braille. Her ongoing education was funded by a businessman friend of author Mark Twain, and after studying at Radcliffe College, Helen graduated in 1904 with a bachelor's degree – she was the first deaf-blind person ever to do so. Keller spent the majority of her adult life campaigning for disability and social issues, and through her own incredible achievements changed the way many people thought about disability.

Eleanor Roosevelt

(1884–1962)

Throughout her life, Eleanor Roosevelt was an advocate for human rights. She is considered to be one of the leading players in the drafting of the UN's 1948 *Universal Declaration of Human Rights*, arguably one of the most important documents of the modern era. Roosevelt was considered somewhat controversial in her time as First Lady – not only did she hold press conferences (previous women in the position had basically been 'silent partners') but also wrote a newspaper column and even publicly disagreed with some of her husband's policies! Eleanor spent her whole life fighting for human rights, leading President Harry Truman to name her 'First Lady of the world'.

Simone de Beauvoir

(1908–1986)

Although she did not consider herself a philosopher, de Beauvoir in fact had a significant influence on feminist theory specifically and existentialism in general. She wrote many novels, essays and monographs on social issues, politics and philosophy, but is perhaps best known for her 1949 work *The Second Sex,* a text which looks at the treatment of women throughout history. The book became the starting point of what is now regarded as the 'second wave' of feminism, and was actually placed on the Vatican's list of prohibited books (to many a sure sign that de Beauvoir was doing something right). One of the book's key points was that men had made women the 'other' in society by applying to them a false sense of mystery; men had then used this as an excuse not to understand problems faced by women; in a similar way to race, class and religion she suggested this was then 'enforced' by those at the top of a society's hierarchy. De Beauvoir highlighted how women who chose not to follow the then domestic norm were looked down upon by society, and in fact criticised Mary Wollstonecraft for her view that men were the ideal to which women should aspire. A number of key concepts in *The Second Sex* became foundations of the 1970s feminist movement, particularly the ideas concerning gender as a social construct. Despite this, de Beauvoir was rather reluctant to call herself a feminist, in fact only doing so in 1972, more than twenty years after the publication of her revolutionary work.

Eleanor Roosevelt in 1947

Susan B Anthony (right) with Elizabeth Cady Stanton

Rosa Parks
(1913–2005)

In the mid-20th Century, America did not treat people of all colours equally. Racial segregation was common, and black people were not given the same rights as their white counterparts. Despite this injustice, many black men and women simply accepted the state of affairs, as the consequences of standing up to the system were more often than not harsh and brutal. However, one famous day a woman by the name of Rosa Parks refused to give up her seat on a bus to a white man. This act was effectively a catalyst that began the modern civil rights movement. Although it took a great deal of time to change America, the direct result of Rosa's defiance was the passing of a law which banned racial segregation on public transport. The true impact of Parks' actions however are much more wide-ranging; despite the many problems America still experiences regarding race, a great deal of progress has been made since the days of racism being directly enshrined in law. Rosa Parks showed that one brave person can take a stance and change the world.

Susan B Anthony
(1920–1906)

Susan Anthony was a key player in the history of women's suffrage. From a young age she was involved in the fight for equal standing and freedom for all, collecting signatures for anti-slavery petitions. Born into a Quaker family, she held core values of decency, fairness and social equality – but rather than just believing in the values and living to them, she wanted to change the world and instil such values in *others* as well. In 1852 she (alongside Elizabeth Cady Stanton) founded the *New York Women's State Temperance Society* after being refused permission to speak at a temperance conference because she was a woman.

Eleven years later she and Elizabeth founded the *Women's Loyal National League*, and collected some 400,000 signatures in support of the abolition of slavery. Three years after that she set up the *American Equal Rights Association* with a focus on equal rights for both women and African Americans. With Stanton and another key figure in women's suffrage – Matilda Joslyn Gage – she wrote the influential six-volume work *History of Women's Suffrage*. Anthony worked tirelessly, giving hundreds of lectures every year, and dedicating her entire life to her cause. In a demonstration against the inequality of the vote, she actually illegally voted in the 1872 presidential election and was arrested for the crime; for this she was fined $100… which she never paid! As a young girl at the start of her campaigning, Anthony was ridiculed by many, even being accused of attempting to destroy the institution of marriage. Yet at the time of her 80th birthday she was celebrated at the White House by invitation of President McKinley. Susan Anthony's contribution to equality for both women and African Americans was celebrated in 1979 when she became the first ever non-fictional woman to be portrayed on US coinage, with her portrait featured on the dollar coin.

BETTY FRIEDAN

(1921–2006)

The Feminine Mystique, written by Betty Friedan in 1963, is considered by many to have kick-started the second wave of 20th Century American feminism. The book considered the traditional role of the American 'homemaker', viewing it as stifling. It revealed the fact that many such housewives felt trapped, and highlighted the fact that Friedan herself had never seen a positive role model who not only kept a family but also worked outside of the home. Other highlights of Friedan's life which she dedicated to the cause of equality include the organisation of the *Women's Strike for Equality* on the 26th August 1970, successful beyond all

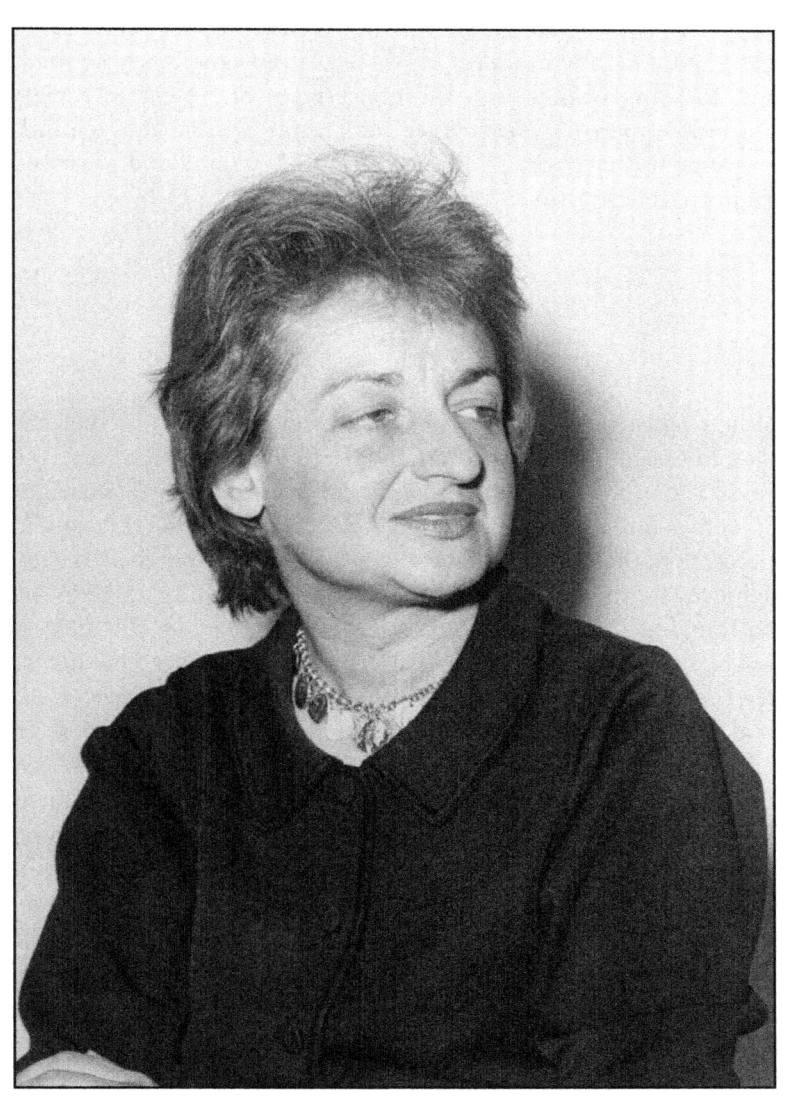

Betty Friedan in 1960

expectations, with a companion march attracting some 50,000 people to New York City and being elected the first president of the *National Organisation for Women*, a movement whose focus was to bring women into the mainstream of American society alongside men. A clear voice of reason within the feminist movement, Betty was often critical of the extreme and polarised factions of feminism.

JANE CAMPBELL
(1959–)

When Jane Campbell was born, her mother was told that she should expect her new-born daughter to die within the year. The reason for this was that Campbell suffers from spinal muscular atrophy, an incurable wasting disease. Despite this awful prediction, that baby is now known as Baroness Campbell, having achieved a great deal in the fight for disability rights. In 1996 she co-founded the *National Centre for Independent Living*, and six years later was appointed chairman of the *Social Care Institute for Excellence*. She also chairs the *British Council of Disabled People* and was commissioner for the *Disability Rights Commission*. In all the positions she has held, Baroness Campbell's focus has been to ensure the organisations have pioneered work in independent living, equal opportunities and civil rights. Her campaigning and day-to-day work has seen the UK make great progress in its treatment of those with disabilities, and even though all acknowledge there is still a long way to go, many people owe their independence to initiatives put in place by Lady Campbell.

Chapter Five

Warfare

Mary Seacole
(1805–1881)

Mary Seacole was born in Jamaica, her father a Scottish soldier and her mother a 'doctress' – a healer who used traditional Caribbean and African herbal remedies. Her mother ran a boarding house (in fact considered to be one of Kingston's best hotels) and it was here that the young Mary learned to practice medicine – first to her dolls, then to pets and eventually to people. Seacole was proud of both her black ancestry and of her Scottish blood, feeling strong affinity for both branches of her family tree. She visited London in the early 1820s before returning to Jamaica in 1826. She worked alongside her mother, both of them occasionally being called to help at the British Army hospital near their home. There were a number of happy years, but 1843 and 1844 were not among them; the family lost most of their boarding house to a fire, then shortly afterwards Mary lost her husband (whom she had married just eight years before). Soon after that, her mother also died. Yet after a period of mourning (during which she did nothing for days on end) Seacole composed herself and assumed management of the boarding house. In 1851 she visited her brother in the country of Panama. Her visit coincided with an outbreak of cholera; Mary's medical knowledge helped her treat the first victim, and when he survived word got around. More and more became infected, and more and more came to sea Mary Seacole. The rich paid for treatment, yet she treated the poor for free – everyone received the same care and attention. When the Crimean War broke out in 1854, Seacole travelled to the Crimea and set up an establishment called the *British Hotel*, in her words a 'mess-table and comfortable quarters for sick and convalescent officers'. Here she treated many British servicemen, and sometimes even visited the front line (which was still under heavy fire) to treat the wounded. Her reputation was similar to that of Florence Nightingale, and many soldiers owed their lives to Mary Seacole. When the war ended, she travelled to England to settle down, but fell into poor health and struggled with money. Thankfully, the press found out about her situation and organised a benefit festival to raise money for her – it was successful, attracting thousands of people grateful for her years of help to the British people. She even published her memoirs: *The Wonderful Adventures of Mrs Seacole in Many Lands.*

1873 Photograph of Mary Seacole

Florence Nightingale circa 1854

Florence Nightingale
(1820–1910)

When she was seventeen, Florence Nightingale believed she had heard the voice of God, who had told her that she had a mission – although she had no idea at the time what that mission actually was. Some nine years later, she found out when she was sent a book that taught her elementary nursing techniques. This led to her volunteering to serve as a nurse in a hospital for soldiers during the Crimean war. Florence had a talent for statistics, and used this to highlight ways that nursing in the army could be improved. Because her diagrams were so easy to understand, they quickly led to a change in procedures, and saved many thousands of lives. As an interesting side-note, some credit her with the invention of the pie-chart! For the rest of her life, Nightingale worked hard to improve the standards of nursing, successfully establishing it as a respectable career for women, and turning hospitals into clean, sanitary places.

Edith Cavell
(1865–1915)

Edith Cavell once said *"I can't stop while there are lives to be saved"*... and she certainly subscribed to this motto. Cavell was an English woman living and working in Belgium when the First World War broke out; her clinic was then taken over by the Red Cross. There, she treated allied and enemy soldiers alike, her view being that *everyone* deserved the highest quality of treatment regardless of their allegiance. In November 1914, the Germans occupied Brussels. Cavell saw it as her duty to assist British soldiers escape from occupied Belgium, helping them make their way to the Netherlands, which was neutral at the time. She helped wounded British and French soldiers (as well as Belgian and French civilians in danger of being called up to fight for the

Nurse Edith Cavell

German army) by hiding them from the authorities whilst they were provided with false papers and given money to make it to the Dutch border. Sadly, she was betrayed to the Germans, who arrested her for aiding the British and French soldiers. She was court-martialled and sentenced to death – a punishment that caused international outrage. Despite protests at the highest level, the Germans carried out her sentence, believing they were right to execute her for the crime of treason. Another quote attributed to Cavell is thus: *"I realize that patriotism is not enough. I must have no hatred or bitterness towards anyone"*. It is a tragedy that her captors did not share the same sentiment.

Flora Sandes
(1876–1956)

When the First World War broke out, Flora Sandes applied to become a nurse, however she was initially rejected due to her lack of qualification in the field. She was however accepted by a St John Ambulance unit raised by an American nurse, and left England for Serbia on the 12th of August 1914. There she joined the Serbian Red Cross, taking up a position as an ambulance worker for the Serbian Army's Second Infantry Regiment. Unfortunately, during a retreat through Albania, Sandes somehow became separated from her unit. Away from home, her companions and in a strange country, the only chance to survive was to enrol as a soldier in the Serbian regiment – it was the only way she could think of to get hold of vital food rations! Sandes quickly advanced to the rank of corporal, and after a number of engagements (including one in which she was wounded by a grenade during hand-to-hand combat) was further promoted to sergeant major. She therefore became the only British woman to serve in the trenches of the First World War – and bravely and successfully so! After the war Sandes was even promoted to Captain, and when she finished her military career had earned a total of seven medals. She published two autobiographies, and travelled the world to lecture on her wartime experiences. In 1941 Germany attacked Yugoslavia and Flora Sandes was recalled to military service, but the invasion was over before she could begin her duties. She eventually returned to England, living in Suffolk until her death in 1956.

Maria Bochkareva

(1889–1920)

Maria Bochkareva was born into a Russian peasant family, and did not have a particularly pleasant early life; her marriage and subsequent relationships were characterised by physically abusive partners. When the First World War broke out, Bochkareva saw this as an opportunity to escape. She therefore joined the Russian Army's 25th Tomsk Reserve Battalion. An initial recruitment of some two thousand volunteers was whittled down to three hundred serious fighting women, of whom Maria was one. This was the *1st Russian Women's Battalion of Death* – a serious and well-trained fighting force. Their first assignment was the Kerensky Offensive at the Western Front, where they performed admirably in battle. Other duties followed, but the unit was eventually disbanded after facing hostility from their counterpart male troops. Russia was in a state of turmoil, and the Bolsheviks detained Bochkareva after she was caught relaying a message to the opposing White Army. She was scheduled to be executed, but a soldier with whom she had served spoke for her and she was granted a stay of execution. She managed to obtain a passport and made her way to America where she was given an audience with President Woodrow Wilson. Maria pleaded with him to do something about the situation in Russia, and – allegedly with tears in his eyes – he said he would do what he could. She returned to Russia in 1919 and attempted to set up a women's medical division of the White Army but was again captured by the Bolsheviks. Maria Bochkareva was then interrogated for four months before being found an 'enemy of the people'. Sadly, this time there was no stay of execution and the sentence was carried out in May 1920.

Мария Бочкарёва (Maria Bochkareva)

Susan Travers

(1909–2003)

During the Second World War, Susan Travers served in the French Red Cross as a nurse and ambulance driver. She realised quickly that she had a passion for serving her country, and decided to dedicate her life to this cause. She spent much of her time in service as a driver and it was in this role where she displayed astonishing courage. At one point she was Foreign Legion Colonel Marie-Pierre Koenig's driver (and, at the time, also his lover). Facing heavy fire and attack from both ground and air, it was decided that the convoy in which they were travelling would have to retreat. Things got even worse when the vehicles were attacked by German machine gun fire and found themselves approaching a minefield. Colonel Koenig suggested they should lead the column, saying "If we go, the rest will follow". Travers therefore put her foot to the floor and raced full pelt, essentially driving blind through the minefield. Her car had been hit by eleven bullets and the brakes had completely stopped working… but she and the rest of the convoy safely reached allied-held territory. As the war continued, Travers drove ambulances, lorries and even a self-propelled anti-tank gun. She was wounded when a car she was in drove over a mine, but recovered to continue the war effort. With such a brave record, after the war Susan Travers was officially accepted into the French Foreign Legion – the only woman ever to have done so. She served in Vietnam during the first Indochina War and was rightly decorated with the *Légion d'Honneur, Croix de Guerre* and the *Médaille Militaire.*

Nancy Wake

(1912–2011)

During the Second World War, Nancy Wake became one of the Allies' most decorated servicewoman. She was a leading figure

Portrait of Susan Travers

Nancy Wake in 1945

in the French Resistance and served in the *Special Operations Executive*, the British unit responsible for espionage, sabotage and reconnaissance. In 1943 Wake had the 'honour' of being the Gestapo's most wanted person, with an incredible five million franc bounty on her head. She had been working for the Maquis in France since the country fell to the Nazis in 1940, becoming a courier for the Resistance, later assisting with the allied escape network. After joining the SOE (having moved to Britain after becoming the Gestapo's most wanted) she actually parachuted *back* into occupied France, becoming liaison between headquarters in London and the local Resistance group. Wake showed complete and utter commitment to the cause of fighting the Nazis, often putting her life at risk to save others. Once she cycled more than three hundred miles through a number of German checkpoints to get replacement codes when her original set had had to be destroyed. She even killed an SS sentry with her bare hands (using a 'judo-chop' technique taught by the SOE) to prevent him from raising an alarm during one important raid. Nancy proved that bravery during wartime was not limited just to the men, even if they did make up the majority of front-line troops.

Princess Noor-un-Nisa Inayat Khan

(1914–1944)

Hailing from a noble Indian Muslim family, Inayat Khan is perhaps one of the more unlikely figures to have become a war hero – however one's background is no indicator of commitment or bravery! Her family had lived in Russia and London before moving to France, where they remained until the country was occupied by German forces; they then fled to England. Although her father had taught her the ways of a pacifist, Khan decided that she had to do *something* to stop the Nazi tyranny, saying that she wished *"some Indians would win high military distinction in this war. If one or two could do something in the Allied service which was very brave and which everybody admired it would help to make a bridge between the English people and the Indians."* She therefore joined the WAAF and was trained as a wireless operator. Whilst on an assignment at a bomber training camp in 1941, she applied for a commission, in her words to 'relieve the boredom' of the work she was doing. She was eventually recruited to join the SOE, and adopted the name Nora Baker. As Inayat spoke fluent French, she was considered a valuable asset and became the first female radio operator to be sent back into occupied France to assist the French Resistance. She was betrayed to the Germans by a double agent, and fought bravely against her arrest so much that some SS officers were afraid of her; she was from then on considered a dangerous prisoner. Khan was interrogated for more than four weeks, but during that period gave the Germans not a single piece of information – although they did find her notebooks which (against regulations) she had made copies of. In September 1944 Khan was transferred to the Dachau concentration camp along with three other SOE agents, where all four were executed with a shot to the back of their heads. Inayat Khan's bravery and contribution to the resistance effort were recognised with a *Croix de Guerre with Silver Star* and a George Cross.

Lyudmila Pavlichenko
(1916–1974)

Lyudmila Pavlichenko saw service during the Second World War as a Soviet sniper, and is generally considered to be not only the most successful female sniper, but also simply one of the top snipers of all time, credited with an astonishing 309 kills. She had learned to shoot after joining a shooting club in Kiev, in her teenage years achieving sharpshooter status whilst working at the city's Arsenal factory. When the Nazis began their invasion of the Soviet Union, Pavlichenko was offered employment in the

Princess Noor-un-Nisa Inayat Khan

1976 Soviet Stamp honouring Lyudmila Pavlichenko

forces as a nurse, but declined, requesting to join the infantry even though women were generally not accepted at the time. She was in fact successful in her application and became one of the Red Army's two thousand female snipers. It was a highly risky position, and three quarters of those women did not live to see the end of the war. In around ten weeks she recorded 187 kills when positioned near Odessa, before seeing the number reach 257 after being moved to the Crimean peninsula. As the number of her confirmed kills neared three hundred, Pavlichenko was wounded by mortar fire. Although she returned to duty after recovering, only a month later she was withdrawn from combat with a total of 309 kills; the Russian military recognised her status and decided she was an important publicity figure, too valuable to risk at the front line. She went on a publicity tour, and became the first Soviet citizen to be received by a US President when she was welcomed to the White House by none other than President Franklin Roosevelt. Although Pavlichenko never returned to combat, she saw out the remainder of the war as an instructor, training other Soviet snipers. The USSR awarded her the *Gold Star of the Hero of the Soviet Union*, and she was even commemorated on one of the country's stamps. Lyudmila is also commemorated in song: folk singer Woody Guthrie wrote 'Miss Pavlichenko' as a tribute to her war record and visit to America.

Eileen Nearne

(1921–2010)

In the Second World War, Eileen Nearne served as a member of the British Special Operations Executive. Based in occupied France she worked as a radio operator under the code-name 'Rose'. Nearne's family had lived in France prior to the war, and she had become fluent in the language. Her unit's role was rather different to that of other SOE teams; whereas they generally focused on sabotage missions, 'Rose' and her colleagues set up a network by the name of *Wizard* which organised sources of finance for the resistance effort. In 1944, her radio transmitter was discovered by the Nazis and she was taken to the Gestapo's Paris headquarters where she was tortured horribly – yet, bravely she kept her secrets, convincing the interrogators that she had been sending messages for a businessman and did not know he was British. She was sent away to spend the remainder of the war in concentration camps, where – refusing to work for the Germans – she was again tortured. Amazingly however, in 1945 she (along with two French girls) escaped the camp, hiding in a forest. The three were captured by the SS, but tricked their captors into releasing them, eventually finding a priest in Leipzig who kept them safe and hidden until US Troops captured the city. Nearne was awarded the *Croix de Guerre* by France, and was made an MBE by King George VI.

Chapter Six
Girls & Young Women

JOAN OF ARC
(1412–1431)

Born in France on the 6th of January 1412, Joan started having religious visions when she was thirteen, which she believed were messages from the Archangel Michael, St Catherine of Alexandria and St Margaret of Antioch. The voices told Joan that her mission was to save France, and after impressing a member of the nobility with an accurate prediction regarding the Battle of Rouvray, she was granted an audience with King Charles VII to whom she relayed her patriotic message. In response to her claims, Joan was given military responsibility, breaking the English siege of Orleans on the 8th of May 1429, and winning a number of subsequent victories. In May 1430 however, Joan was captured in battle and sold to the English for 10,000 crowns. Put on trial for sorcery and heresy, Joan d'Arc was found guilty and burned at the stake. Almost five hundred years later, she was declared a saint by the Catholic Church.

POCAHONTAS
(1596–1617)

In December 1607, Captain John Smith, an English settler who had arrived in Virginia seven months prior, was exploring the Chickahominy river when he was captured by Tsenacommacah Indians and was brought to the home of Powhatan, the leader of an alliance of some thirty small groups of Indians. According to one version of events told by Smith (he rather confused things by stating slightly differing accounts) he was due to be executed via a blow from Powhatan's axe when at the last minute one of the chief's daughters had placed her head upon his in order to save him (although some historians have since speculated the event may not have been a planned execution, but a 'rebirth' ritual). After this, the girl – named *Pocahontas* – befriended Smith, and

Joan of Arc as depicted in an illustration from a 1505 manuscript.

he returned to England some time in 1609. A year or so afterwards and Pocahontas was captured by another band of English settlers, who kept her after their original ransom demands to her father had not been satisfied. During the time she was held by the English, Pocahontas was Christened with a new name (Rebecca) and taught their language. When violence broke out once again between the English and her tribe, she was permitted to speak to her father in a diplomatic role; she apparently told him in one meeting that she preferred to remain with the English rather than return home. At some point, 'Rebecca' met John Rolfe, a farmer who had lost his wife and child on the journey to Virginia; the two married – although we do not know if she was as keen on the union as he was! Their partnership did however bring peace to the Anglo-Indian conflict and they lived on Rolfe's farm for two years together. It was later decided that she should be brought back to England as an example of a 'tamed savage' and on doing so she became somewhat famous – although she was treated as a kind of curiosity. By chance, she did actually encounter John Smith at a social gathering in 1617, and he wrote that she seemed 'uncontent' with her life. So much of Pocahontas's story is difficult to separate into truth and myth, especially the 'romance' between her and Smith. It has been romanticized over the years – usually with the slightly dubious 'moral' being that 'savages can be tamed' based on the young girl's choice to remain with her English captors.

Eliza Lucas

(1722–1793)

Born in Antigua into a rich family, Eliza Lucas moved with her family to the British Colony of South Carolina in 1738. There, they owned several plantations totalling more than two thousand acres. An inquisitive child, Eliza was encouraged by her father to learn whatever she wanted, and was given full access to the family library. Not only did Eliza herself learn a great deal from the library, but she also used her knowledge to teach others –

particularly the slave children on the plantations; she hoped that they would also help to educate their peers. After being encouraged to study various plants by her father (with a view to expanding the plantations' offerings) she suggested they try growing indigo, a valuable crop but one which had not been successfully cultivated outside of the West Indies. In 1739 she – along with the help of slaves who had experience of indigo in their native lands – developed a new strain of the plant which could grow well in the South Carolina soil. Figuring out a way to ship the dye over to England, Eliza Lucas had ended England's grudging reliance on French indigo, and therefore became a wealthy and successful businesswoman before the age of 21, with her indigo strain becoming colonial South Carolina's most important cash crop. Many years after her death, Lucas became the first woman to be inducted into the South Carolina business hall of fame.

Sybil Ludington

(1761–1839)

The night of April 26th, 1777 saw Sybil Ludington go down in history as a heroine of the American Revolutionary War. In similar circumstances to Paul Revere, Ludington rode through the night to alert her father's militiamen that the British were coming – although in fact her ride was twice as long as that of Revere's! She was just sixteen when she made her forty-mile trek on a horse called Star, and even defended herself with a stick against a highwayman who accosted her during the epic journey. Sybil's heroic effort ensured that some four hundred men were ready to fight, and although they could not save Danbury, Connecticut, they did manage to drive the British general back to New York's Long Island Sound. Although General George Washington congratulated Sybil, her story was not particularly well remembered, and it was not recorded in print until over a hundred years after the event.

Sacajawea
(1788–1812)

In 1804 Meriwether Lewis and William Clark set out on an expedition to cross what is today the western part of the United States, with the main aims being to map what was then newly acquired territory, to find a practical route to the Pacific coast, and to establish an American presence before Britain or other European powers could claim it. In November that year, Lewis and Clark built Fort Mandan in the upper Missouri river area, and there hired a French-Canadian trapper called Toussaint Charbonneau as their interpreter. Charbonneau had bought a girl called Sacajawea from the *Hidatsa* Indians; she was a *Shoshone* – enemies of the Hidatsa – and had been captured when she was just twelve years old. She became one of Charbonneau's wives, and even though she was pregnant with her first child, she also joined her husband on Lewis and Clark's expedition – the explorers felt that her knowledge of the Shoshone language would help them during their journey. If it wasn't for Sacajawea, it is likely the expedition would not have been the success that it was. She helped keep the explorers alive through her knowledge of edible plants, and even saved the cargo from a boat full of supplies that capsized. At one point, the group encountered a band of Shoshone Indians, and by chance their leader was Sacajawea's brother! She helped Lewis and Clark negotiate the purchase of horses from her brother's men (which allowed them to cross the Rocky Mountains), and chose to remain with the explorers for the remainder of their journey. Despite her young age and the fact that she was carrying her new-born child for the majority of the expedition, Sacajawea proved that she was a knowledgeable and intelligent guide, and it is likely that the history of the world would be very different had she not helped the Corps of Discovery.

Statue of Sacajawea in Portland, Oregon

Portrait and Signature of Ernestine Rose

ERNESTINE ROSE
(1810–1892)

Ernestine Rose was born in Poland, the daughter of a wealthy rabbi. When she was sixteen, her mother (herself from a rich background) died. Not long afterwards, Ernestine's father decided she should be married and he betrothed her to one of his friends. She did not want to marry a man whom she did not love, and that she had not herself chosen. Ernestine begged the man to release her from the betrothal, but he refused – amongst other reasons he stood to share in the rather large inheritance she had recently been given. Despite her young age – and it being against the customs of the time – Rose took her case to the courts, and they ruled in her favour; the first instance of a period of transition within the legal system that, over time, ensured women had a say in to whom they would be wed. For the rest of her life, Ernestine fought for human rights. After moving to England (she had discovered her father had remarried a sixteen-year-old girl and decided to leave home) she helped her friend Robert Owen establish the *Association of All Classes of All Nations*, a group that fought for human rights and equality for all. Rose fell in love and married a jeweller and they moved to the United States. There she travelled from state to state, speaking out against slavery. She met with plenty of resistance, with one southern slaveholder telling her that if she had been a man he would have her *"tarred and feathered"*; in another instance a local paper called her a *"female atheist, a thousand times below a prostitute"*! She joined forces with women such as Elizabeth Cady Stanton, Susan B. Anthony and others to fight for abolition and women's rights. In 1854 Ernestine was elected president of the *National Women's Rights Convention*; twenty years later she travelled to England and spoke at a women's suffrage conference. Whilst her first foray into the human rights movement was essentially for her own protection, her entire life was spent trying to help others and she should be remembered as an important and influential figure in an age of massive change.

CYNTHIA ANN PARKER
(1825–1871)

In 1836, a *Comanche* war band massacred the Parker family settlement and kidnapped the then ten-year-old Cynthia. Giving her the name *Naduah* (sometimes written as *Narua*) meaning 'someone found', she was raised by the Comanche tribe for 24 years, completely forgoing her American ways – even marrying a tribal chieftain with whom she had three children (including the last free Comanche chief, Quanah Parker). When she was 34, Naduah was recaptured by the Texas Rangers but insisted that her home was with her tribe, and refused to adjust to life in white society. More than once she attempted to escape and return to her Native American family, but was always brought back to Texas. White Americans saw her recapture as something positive – a kind of redemption – yet Cynthia never saw it this way; in her eyes she had been removed from her chosen way of life. A few years later, when Cynthia lost the only child she still had contact with, she chose to forego food and water, and died soon afterwards.

ANNE FRANK
(1929–1945)

in 1933, Anne Frank's Jewish family moved to Holland to escape from the Nazis who were persecuting people of their faith. By 1942, the Nazis had invaded and were occupying the country and Anne's entire family went into hiding in a secret annex in an attic above her father's office. During this time, Anne wrote into a diary that she had been given for her thirteenth birthday. In 1944, the family were betrayed to the Nazis and all eight were sent to a concentration camp. Anne died of typhus in March 1945. After the war, Anne's diary was published by her father, who was the only member of the family to survive; it is a truly harrowing read and one that is required reading for many educational systems across the world.

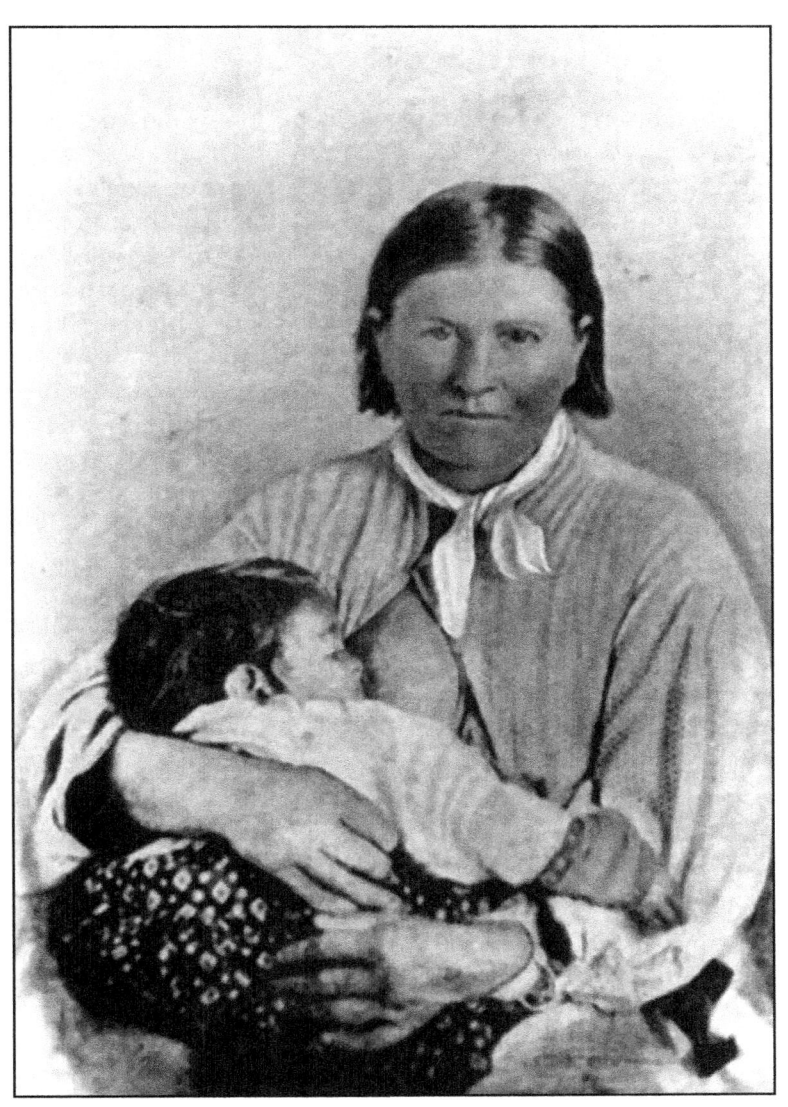
Photograph of Cynthia Ann Parker taken in 1861

Ruby Bridges
(1954–)

When Ruby bridges was four years old, her family moved to New Orleans. It was a time of racial division in America, and many institutions were segregated based on the colour of people's skin. After living in New Orleans for two years, Ruby's family responded to a request from the *National Association for the Advancement of Colored People* who were looking for volunteers to participate in a project to integrate the city's school system. Although Ruby's father was at first unsure, her mother persuaded him it was an important step for the advancement of African-American rights, and he agreed to allow his daughter to attend a previously whites-only school. On the first day of school, a large crowd of people gathered outside the building, shouting and throwing objects at Ruby and her parents as she walked towards it – yet Ruby did not cry nor whimper, she bravely marched onwards in defiance of those who taunted her. When she arrived at the school, the parents of the white children pulled them out of class, and all of the teachers but one refused to have a black child in their class. Ruby's first day at school was spent barricaded in the principal's office. On the second day however, a white minister walked his daughter through the protesting mob (saying he *"just wanted the privilege of taking his child to school"*) and gradually the protests subsided – although Ruby was only able to eat food that she brought in from home as one committed protester regularly shouted that she was going to poison her. Ruby has since said that the one thing that scared her more than the shouting and the throwing was a particular woman who was protesting by carrying a wooden coffin with a black doll laying inside it – but Ruby tells of how she managed to overcome her fear by praying as she walked past the awful effigy. The Bridges family suffered for their brave decision; Ruby's father was fired from his job and the supermarket they previously shopped at refused to serve them. Yet others in the community showed support; one offered her father a new job, and many others volunteered to watch over Ruby and to guard her family's home in case of attack. It would have been easy – and understandable – for Ruby to have chosen not to face such a terrible daily onslaught, but her bravery and persistence helped to advance rights for African-Americans significantly. Today, Ruby is chair of her own foundation which promotes the values of tolerance, respect and appreciation of all differences.

Ruby Bridges being escorted by US Marshals

Malala Yousafzai
(1997–)

Malala Yousafzai's family had been running a chain of school in Pakistan for many years, mainly based in a province in the North West of the country, where the local Taliban regularly banned girls from attending school. In 2009 at the age of eleven, Malala wrote a blog under a pseudonym for the BBC, which focused on her life under Taliban rule and her views of the promotion of women's education. The next year, the *New York Times* filmed a documentary about her life and as the Pakistani military gradually fought the Taliban out of the region, Malala began to rise in prominence, giving interviews for a number of publications and media channels, always talking about the importance of education for young girls. In 2012, she had just boarded her school bus when a gunman, identifying her by asking her name, shot her three times from close range with a pistol. Although she was close to death, Malala somehow managed to survive, and once she was outside of the critical condition phase was flown to a hospital in the UK. Back in Pakistan, a group of fifty Muslim Clerics issued a *fatwa* against her attempted murderers, but the Taliban answered back, stating they still intended to kill both Malala and her father. Having almost completely recovered physically, Yousafzai has gone on to speak around the world about her experience and her belief in education, even being named one of the world's one hundred most influential people. She has gained respect from the vast majority of people in the world for speaking out against oppression, believing in a cause so strongly that it enables her to stand up against those who want to silence her in the worst possible way. In 2015 at the age of just seventeen, Malala won the Nobel peace prize, becoming the award's youngest ever recipient.

Chapter Seven
Sport

Charlotte Dod
(1871–1960)

In 1887, Lottie Dod (as she was known) won that year's Wimbledon Ladies' singles Championship, and to this day remains the youngest person ever to have done so. Lottie went on to repeat the achievement another *four times* throughout an amazing career. Incredibly, tennis was not the only sport in which she competed; she was also a participant in golf (winning the British Ladies Championship), archery (winning silver at the 1908 Olympics) and hockey (playing twice for the England women's team). Incredibly, in the final of the 1888 Wimbledon championship, Lottie – christened 'Little Wonder' by the press – actually had a handicap (of 15) imposed on her despite the tournament supposedly being 'open'! Of course, she still managed to win. In addition to her summer sports, Lottie also rode the toboggan at the world famous Cresta Run, passed the prestigious St Moritz Skating test and conquered two mountains over 4000m in height. Lottie is considered by the *Guinness Book of Records* to be – alongside Babe Didrikson Zaharias – one of the two most versatile female athletes of all time.

Annette Kellermann
(1887–1975)

Some people know Annette Kellermann as the first major actress ever to appear nude in a Hollywood film, however she achieved a great deal more than that in her life. She was almost solely responsible for a huge shift in fashion; traditionally women had always worn 'pantaloon'-style bathing suits, but Kellermann popularised the one-piece costume. In the early 1900s this was a highly controversial step; in fact in 1907 she was actually arrested for indecency for simply wearing a one-piece costume from her

Charlotte Dod, Aged 20

Annette Kellermann in 1907

own swimwear line! Kellermann was a champion swimmer, winning regional competitions at 100 yards and one mile distances. Her natural ability in the water led to her performing in a number of aquatic shows, including swimming with fish in a glass aquarium and sensational high-dive stunts. Perhaps her most lasting legacy however is that Annette popularised synchronised swimming as a sport after audiences experienced her performing the first ever water ballet at the New York Hippodrome – a glass tank was constructed specially for the event. The film in which Kellermann appeared nude was called *A Daughter of the Gods* and was released in 1916; it was also the first million-dollar film production. Sadly for fans and film historians, it is believed that no complete copies of the film exist today.

Babe Didrikson Zaharias
(1911–1956)

Winning ten major golf tournaments would be enough for some people – but not for Babe Zaharias. In addition to these LPGA majors, she also proved highly successful in basketball and a range of track & field events. At the 1932 Olympics, Babe took the 80 metre hurdles gold medal with a world record time of 11.7 seconds, threw a gold medal-winning world record 43.69 metres in the Javelin, and won a silver medal in the high jump – she jumped the same height as the gold medal winner, but was ruled to have jumped with an 'improper technique'. Zaharias led her basketball team to win the 1931 AAU Basketball Championship, and played pocket billiards at competition level. In addition to her medal-winning achievements, Babe was also an excellent baseball and softball player, an expert diver, an accomplished roller-skater, a fierce bowler and even the winner of a state-wide sewing competition. Alongside Lottie Dod, Babe is considered one of the two greatest female athletes of all time.

Sonja Henie
(1912–1969)

Sonja Henie holds the record of having won more Olympic and World figure skating titles than any other woman. At the age of just fourteen, Sonja won the 1927 World Figure Skating Championships, and went on to win the next *nine* – an unprecedented run of success. As her skating career was coming to an end in 1936, Henie began to focus on the dream she had as a young girl – she wanted to become a Hollywood star. After her father had orchestrated an ice show in Los Angeles to demonstrate her many talents, she was signed to Twentieth Century Fox. Her first film – *One in a Million* – was a huge success and Henie went on to be one of Hollywood's highest paid actresses. During her skating days, Sonja had enjoyed performing in Germany, and was one of Hitler's favourite participants. She once greeted Hitler with a Nazi salute and was denounced by the press in her home country of Norway. Henie was close to many senior Nazis; Goebbels himself arranged for the distribution of *One in a Million* in Germany. Some of Henie's countrymen condemned her for not speaking out against the Nazis, however she *did* become an American citizen, and contribute to the allied war effort by taking part in USO shows for the troops. After the war, she continued to perform in shows on ice and remained a popular figure for many years. As well as being a member of both the World Figure Skating and Women's Sports Halls of Fame, Sonja also has her own star on the Hollywood 'Walk of Fame'.

Fanny Blankers-Koen
(1918–2004)

Fanny Blankers-Koen, a Dutch athlete, is generally considered to be the woman who proved that age and motherhood were no barrier to success on the sports field. A multidisciplinary

Sonja Henie at the 1936 Olympics

competitor, Fanny set an astonishing number of world records and could easily have been the most successful athlete of all time had the Second World War not seen a break in international competition. In total Fanny set (or tied) twelve different world records including those in the long jump, high jump, hurdles and sprinting. She first competed in the Olympics in 1936, and despite the fact she had only been involved in athletics for a single year she still came away with bronze medals in the 100 and 200 metre events. After the war ended, the next Olympics were held in London in 1948. Blankers-Koen utterly dominated her events, and was in fact the most successful athlete in the whole of the games – she took home no fewer than four gold medals. The facts that this was achieved at the age of thirty, and that she had given birth to two children showed the world that motherhood was no barrier to success, and earned Fanny the nickname of 'the flying housewife'. The IAAF considers Fanny to be the female athlete of the 20th century, and it is not difficult to see why. An annual athletics event is still held in Fanny's honour in the Dutch city of Hengelo.

Alice Coachman
(1923–2014)

Raised in the American south, Alice, a young and fit athletic black girl, was subjected to segregation at every turn. She was not permitted to access any of the training facilities (which were only for the use of whites) and was unwelcome at any organised sports events. Undeterred, Alice constructed equipment from odds and ends she found around her home and used it to practice her jumping skills; for fitness training she ran barefoot along the dirt roads that streaked through her neighbourhood. When Alice attended high school, she was finally able to join a track team and was quickly noticed by senior athletic figures, who gave her a scholarship to her local Preparatory school. Whilst there, she won national championships in a number of disciplines, although the high jump was always her main focus. Alice was in her prime when war broke out, which meant there were no Olympic games held in 1940 nor in 1944. In 1948 however, Alice attended the London games, winning a gold medal in the high jump – the only American woman to win a gold medal that year. This achievement meant that she became the first ever black woman to have won an Olympic gold medal. On returning to the States, Alice became somewhat of a celebrity and was signed up by Coca Cola to endorse their products, making her the first African American women to endorse an international product; she was featured on billboards with Jesse Owens, whose Olympic feat had been achieved twelve years before hers. If it were not for the war, many commentators believe that Alice could easily have been the greatest female athlete of all time, based on her success in a wide range of events at national level during the war years. In 1975 Alice was inducted into the USA Track and Field Hall of Fame, and was honoured at the 1996 Atlanta Olympics as one of the one hundred greatest Olympians of all time.

LARISSA LATYNINA
(1934–)

Larissa Latynina holds the record for the most Olympic gold medals won by any gymnast – nine in total. In total Larissa won eighteen Olympic medals, a record which stood from 1964 to 2012 when it was exceeded by Michael Phelps. From 1956 until 1964, Larissa was the star of the gymnastic events at each Olympic Games, and it was her success in these events which saw the Soviet Union emerge as a dominant force in world gymnastics. In the 1958 World Championships, Latynina won five of the six disciplines in which she competed, even though she was four months pregnant at the time. Alongside a more recent superstar – Simone Biles – Larissa is one of only two female gymnasts to have won an event final gold, an all-round gold *and* a team gold model at the same Olympics – although Larissa actually achieved this feat twice (in 1956 and 1960). After retiring from competing herself, Latynina became the Soviet gymnastics coach, and under her leadership the women's team won gold in 1968, 1972 and 1976 (she retired in 1977). In 1998 Larissa was inducted into the International Gymnastics Hall of Fame and is remembered as one of the greatest gymnasts ever to have competed at international level.

Larissa Latynina (left) in 1964

Billie Jean King
(1943–)

Throughout her career in tennis, Billie Jean King won an incredible 39 Grand Slam titles. Her contribution to sport is much greater than just these achievements though; a male player by the name of Bobby Riggs had declared the women's game as 'inferior', and stated that although he had now retired from professional tennis (at this point he was 55) he could *still* beat any of the top female players. The first female player to take him up on the wager was Margaret Court; she lost 6-2 6-1. After Riggs continued to taunt the female players, King accepted a lucrative financial offer to play him in a nationally televised match. The game, dubbed the 'Battle of the Sexes' was in Riggs's favour initially, but King's strategy was the better one and she won the match 6-1, 6-3, 6-3, proving forever that female sports stars were not inferior to their male counterparts.

Martina Navratilova
(1956–)

The only person to have held the number one position in both singles *and* doubles tennis for more than two hundred weeks, Martina Navratilova holds the records for both the most singles titles (at 167) and doubles titles (177) in the modern era. In one five-year period (between 1982 and 1986) Navratilova won 428 of the 442 singles matches in which she played, making it the most dominant period ever recorded in the sport. Martina holds a huge number of statistical records, including being the only woman to have reached nineteen consecutive major semi-finals; she was ranked in the top ten from 1975 for an astonishing twenty consecutive years, and won her last major title (the US Open doubles event) in 2006 – more than thirty years after her first Grand Slam victory. Navratilova has been a vocal campaigner for human and animal rights, and has achieved a great deal in promoting gay rights, in 2000 being given a *National Equality* award by the *Human Rights Campaign*.

JACKIE JOYNER-KERSEE
(1962–)

As a young girl, Jackie Joyner-Kersee saw a film about Babe Zaharias and was inspired to compete in a range of track and field events. Natural talent combined with dedication and perseverance saw Jackie develop into a hugely successful athlete, and she eventually competed at four different Olympic Games, winning three gold medals, one silver and two bronze. She is generally considered to be one of the greatest heptathletes in history – in fact *Sports Illustrated for Women* named her as the greatest female athlete of all time, even ahead of the woman who inspired her, Babe Zaharias. After her Olympic career (which lasted from 1984 all the way through to 1996) ended, Joyner-Kersee has dedicated her life to helping others; she established her own foundation which provides athletic tuition and life support to poorer families and was also a founding member of the charity Athletes for Hope. At the time of writing, Jackie still holds the world record in the heptathlon – in fact her domination of the sport is so complete that she holds *all* of the top *six* points records.

Chapter Eight
Literature

1873 Portrait of Jane Austen

Jane Austen
(1775–1817)

Jane Austen's contribution to the world of literature was her collection of six major novels which essentially saw the transition from the sensitive, emotional novels of the late 18th century to the realism of the early 19th century. Even today, two hundred years later, her novels are rarely (if ever) out of print, and she is studied far and wide as one of the leading figures of English literature. Despite all of this, she did *not* achieve significant fame during her lifetime – in fact, her novels were first publishing anonymously. Sadly, at the peak of her writing career, Austen, aged 41, fell ill and died; modern-day thinking is that she suffered from Addison's disease. It was only after her death that her brother Henry revealed to the public that Jane had been the author. Over time, her body of work was appreciated more and more, and with the advent of moving pictures came adaptations of her novels – even today Austen's books are commonly turned into films and TV series. Her work is full of astute observations that respectfully question (and even poke fun at) the social graces and customs of the period in which she lived, yet they remain as relevant today as they were when first written.

Mary Shelley
(1797–1851)

There can be few people today who have not heard of *Frankenstein*, even if they have not necessarily read the original work. What has made the story so enduring? The answer is perhaps that it is widely considered to be the first ever science fiction work ever written. In 1816, Mary and her partner Percy Shelley travelled to Lake Geneva where they spent the summer with the poet Lord Byron and his young physician. They spent the weeks writing, talking and boating on the lake – when the weather was good… but it was a poor summer and much time was spent inside. One night, a few days after it bad been suggested the members of the group should write a ghost story, Mary had what she described as a 'waking dream', a vision of a man working on a creation which appeared to stir briefly with life. She took this idea, initially planning to work it into a short story, but – encouraged by Percy Shelley – she turned it into a full novel – of course, Frankenstein – which was published two years later. Although she spent the rest of her life writing further novels, it is her first novel which remains to this day her most popular, although in the last few decades, her other works have been re-appraised and are increasingly considered important contributions to English literature.

Mary Anne Evans
(1819–1880)

In Victorian England, the name 'Mary Anne Evans' would have meant very little, but 'George Elliot' would have certainly been recognised – after all, 'he' had written *The Mill on the Floss* in 1860, and a number of other successful novels which were praised for both their realism and insight into human psychology. Actually, these two were one and the same – George Elliot was Mary's pen name. She explained that she used a male pen name to ensure that her works would be taken seriously in an age where woman were considered to be second-class. Female authors were published at the time – and in fact in her own right Mary *was* known as an editor and critic – yet the majority of fiction written by women was considered (by Mary) to be light-hearted romance, whereas her aim was to address wider social issues. Interestingly, Evans was championed by Virginia Woolf, who described her novels as 'written for grown-up people'. They generally featured depictions of rural Victorian society, yet being character-focused contained themes relevant to any era. Evans believed there was great interest to be had from the everyday lives of 'ordinary' people, and her novel *Middlemarch* is considered by some (including Martin Amis) as the greatest novel in the English language.

Mary Anne Evans in 1865

A Photograph of Nellie Bly from 1890

NELLIE BLY
(1864–1922)

The risks that some journalists take and the lengths they go to perhaps goes unnoticed nowadays, however it was Nellie Bly who pioneered the idea of putting herself right in the action to give her readers the most incredible stories. In journalistic circles, Bly is best known for her book *Ten Days in a Mad-House*. There had been rumours of brutality, neglect and mistreatment of women at the Women's Lunatic Asylum situated on an island in New York City's East River; Bly therefore underwent an undercover assignment for the *New York World* in which she feigned insanity in order to investigate and report on the institution. After successfully fooling a court that she was insane (she had previously checked into a boarding house and acted strangely enough for the proprietors to call the police in) she was taken to the institution where she experienced shocking treatment; the food was not fit for animals, the water dirty and undrinkable; rats infested the entire hospital and patients were forced to sit in freezing rooms on hard benches with no protection from the elements. Nurses regularly beat the patients and poured cold water over their heads as a substitute for bathing. Bly was convinced that a number of the patients were actually sane, and after ten days, was released after the truth about her mission was explained by her newspaper. Soon afterwards she published the story of her experiences and it absolutely shocked the public. As a direct result, a grand jury investigation was launched and care of those with mental issues was drastically improved. In addition to this expose, for another story, Nellie Bly turned the book *Around the World in Eighty Days* into a factual story, by undertaking a 24,899-mile journey around the world (which actually lasted 72 days) setting a world record in the process. In her later years, Bly reported from the Eastern Front during the First World War and wrote articles about women's suffrage. Nellie Bly changed the entire nature of journalism whilst also championing women's rights.

Virginia Woolf
(1882-1941)

Considered one of the foremost modernists of the 20th century, Virginia Woolf is known for her free-form, non-linear style of prose. She experimented with various literary tools in her novels, notably dream-states and unusual narrative perspectives. Her writings addressed issues important to her heart, such as feminism, homosexuality and mental illness – the latter of these particularly relevant as today's scholars believe Woolf may have herself suffered from bipolar disorder. Woolf was regularly welcomed to speak at academic institutions and was well respected as an academic, an innovative thinker and an exceptional writer. Although she was certainly popular in her own time, it was the 1970s which saw a resurgence of interest in her writings, with aspects of her work ringing true for the feminist movement of the era once again. At the age of 59, Woolf filled her pockets with stones and walked into the River Ouse; it is believed she committed suicide during a bipolar episode after her London home was bombed out during the Blitz and her Jewish husband faced the prospect of being caught and imprisoned by the Nazis.

Agatha Christie
(1890-1976)

With her collected works selling some two billion copies worldwide, Agatha Christie is considered by the *Guinness Book of World Records* to be the best-selling novelist of all time. In fact, in terms of sales ranking, her books only come behind those of Shakespeare and the Bible! Her books have been translated into over one hundred different languages, making Christie the most widely-read author in the world. Her most popular book is *And Then There Were None*, which is the world's best-selling mystery novel and one of the highest-selling books ever. She is also remembered for her play *The Mousetrap*, a West-end fixture since it was first performed, and still regarded as one of the best evenings one can attend in theatre. The sheer popularity of Christie's work means that she will forever be remembered as one of the greatest authors of all time.

Virginia Woolf in 1927

Maya Angelou at President Clinton's Inauguration

Maya Angelou
(1928–2014)

In 1969, Maya Angelou published an autobiography focusing on her experiences up to the age of seventeen called *I Know Why the Caged Bird Sings*, and it became the first non-fiction bestseller by an African-American woman. Angelou went on to write another six such autobiographies; as well as championing black culture, the books address themes such as identity and family as well as covering ground such as racism, and detailing Angelou's extensive travels. Maya Angelou also wrote a number of essays, poems, plays, television shows and movies. Throughout her life she was a civil rights activist and was considered as a spokesperson for many black citizens of America and even further afield. Angelou was close to Martin Luther King, Jr.; he was in fact assassinated on her 40th birthday, a fact that meant she did not celebrate the day for many years afterwards. From her fifties all the way through until her eighties, Angelou spoke at almost one hundred appearances a year on the lecture circuit, ensuring that a large number of people were able to experience her insights into life and her hope that the world would one day be a place where all were considered equal.

Germaine Greer
(1939–)

Often controversial, Germaine Greer is the author of the book *The Female Eunuch*, an important feminist work that explores the idea of society's imposition of certain norms on women's behaviour, and of continual female oppression. Regarding her controversy, Germaine stated *'The more people we annoy, the more we know we're doing it right'*. She says that her aim is not equality with men, but liberation of women; essentially she does not see men's achievements as the *limit* of women's potential. In addition to a focus on feminism, Greer has also championed environmental and equality-based causes.

Danielle Steel
(1947–)

The fourth bestselling author of all time (according to generally reliable sources), Steel was brought up in a well-to-do family; from an early age she attended dinner parties thrown by her parents, giving her the opportunity to observe at close hand the lives of the rich and powerful. Although some critics describe Steel's novels as 'formulaic' (they often focus on over-the-top characters facing some sort of crisis which threatens their relationship) her novels address tough issues such as illness, death, divorce and even suicide and therefore are considered important in helping everyday men and women understand and empathise with problems that they may not necessarily have first-hand experience with. Outside of her literary work, Steel raises money for charities in the mental health field.

J.K. Rowling
(1965–)

The *Harry Potter* series has sold so many copies that it has actually been credited with leading a revival in children's reading. The first book in the series was written by Rowling when she was a single mother struggling to make ends meet, but with her perseverance she has turned the series into one of the most successful of all time. In addition to simply giving millions of children and adults enormous pleasure from reading her books, J.K. Rowling has used her wealth to assist many causes close to her heart, including those such as anti-poverty, multiple sclerosis and helping institutionalised children.

Chapter Nine
Science & Technology

Jeanne Baret
(1740–1807)

Jeanne Baret's 'better-known' achievement is that she was the first woman to circumnavigate the world. In itself this is worthy of recognition, however it is the *reason* that she did this that is most interesting when considering her contribution to science. Baret was a botanist and her love of the field was what made her decide to risk life and limb in expanding her research. She thus disguised herself as a man – calling herself Jean Baret – and signed up for France's first attempt at circumnavigating the globe. It was on this voyage that she worked 'under' Philibert Commerson, the expedition's chief botanist. The voyage was long and arduous but ultimately successful; some six thousand specimens were brought back to the French National Herbarium. Out of these, around seventy bear the name of Commerson in his honour. However, history does not always make the truth clear to us. In actual fact, Commerson suffered from long bouts of ill health, and was regularly unable to collect the specimens, often staying in his ship's bunk rather than venture deep into uncharted territory to collect new, amazing plants and suchlike. In fact, it was the intrepid Baret who did so – yet not a single specimen carried her name. It was only in recent times that Jeanne Baret's contribution to the science of botany has been more widely recognised, including the naming of *Solanum baretiae* in her honour.

Ada Lovelace
(1815–1852)

In computing circles, Ada Lovelace is generally referred to as the first ever computer programmer. Although its potential was not really recognised at the time, Charles Babbage's analytical engine is today thought of as being the world's first computer. It was a fascinating machine, and the history of the world would surely

Portrait of Ada Lovelace from 1836

be very different had it received the funding and development Babbage desperately needed. Ada Lovelace first came into contact with Babbage when she was asked to translate a French write-up of a lecture he delivered back into English. Over a period of a year, she worked closely with the inventor to ensure her translation was accurate and correct in every aspect; she also decided to enhance the transcript with notes of her own. In one of her notes, she described an algorithm that would allow the analytical engine to calculate Bernoulli numbers (an important series in number theory) which, as a specifically-tailored algorithm for a programmable device, can certainly be considered as the first ever computer program. This wasn't just a 'lucky strike' either – she saw the *full* potential of the analytical engine, understanding its ability to be adapted for abstract operational purposes. Whilst some historians disagree about the extent to which Lovelace contributed (they argue that her notes are essentially dictations directly from Babbage) almost everyone agrees on one thing – that she spotted and solved the first 'bug' in programming – having noted and corrected an error in one set of Babbage's calculations.

Marie Curie

(1867–1934)

Not only was Marie Curie the first woman to receive the Nobel Prize, but she was also the first person to win the prize for two separate categories – Physics in 1903 and Chemistry in 1911. Her research into radioactivity (which ultimately killed her) had a massive impact on the human race, on the one hand leading to the development of nuclear weapons, on the other hand saving lives after developing the first ever X-ray machines. Curie actually coined the phrase *radioactivity*, and as part of her research into the science discovered two elements – *polonium* and *radium*. Thanks to Marie Curie, the X-ray machine helped treat wounded soldiers in the First World War, yet it was her exposure to the emissions of such machines – and her habit of carrying test tubes of radioactive material in her pockets – that eventually led to her death in France at the age of 66.

Marie Curie in 1911

Lise Meitner with Otto Hahn

LISE MEITNER
(1878–1968)

Lise Meitner could easily be considered to have contributed to nuclear research as much even as Marie Curie. Whilst working with Otto Hahn, Meitner led a small group of scientists whose greatest achievement was the discovery of nuclear fission in uranium. Meitner, along with Otto Frisch, realised that the process of fission must coincide with a huge release of energy; this insight essentially led to the development of nuclear weapons, and with their deployment against Japan, the end of the Second World War and the beginning of the nuclear age. Of course, one must also credit Meitner that the same discovery also led to the generation of power by nuclear reactors which offered humankind an alternative to the burning of fossil fuels in order to generate energy. Whilst the Nobel Prize for chemistry was given to her partner in science Otto Hahn, Meitner's contribution – as is the story with so many other women in this book – was ignored. In more recent times, Meitner's efforts have begun to be more widely recognised, and she has been awarded a number of posthumous honours; perhaps the most important being the rare accolade of having a chemical element being named after her – number 109 is now called *meitnerium* in recognition of Lise Meitner's vital contribution to modern science.

CECILIA PAYNE
(1900–1979)

After hearing a lecture at the University of Cambridge given by Sir Arthur Eddington about an expedition he took to the island of Principe (which confirmed Einstein's theory of general relativity), Cecilia Payne was inspired to become an astronomer. Her work in that field is considered amongst the most important ever conducted, and her 1925 Ph.D. thesis is said by some to be the

Cecilia Payne

most brilliant ever written in astronomy. Payne used the spectral lines of different elements in conjunction with an equation discovered by an Indian astrophysicist called Meghnad Saha to firmly establish that the spectral sequence of stars corresponded to their stellar temperatures. Furthermore she determined that stars were mainly composed of hydrogen and helium, as opposed to a similar composition of that of the earth, which is what other leading astronomers of the day believed. On accepting her *Henry Norris Russell Prize* from the *American Astronomical Society* for her important work, Cecilia said *"The reward of the young scientist is the emotional thrill of being the first person in the history of the world to see something or to understand something. Nothing can compare with that experience... The reward of the old scientist is the sense of having seen a vague sketch grow into a masterly landscape."*

Grace Hopper
(1906-1992)

There are in fact plenty more women involved in the history of computing than many people realise. One of the great contributors is surely Grace Hopper, an American computer scientist. Her best-known achievements are that she invented the first ever compiler for a computer programming language and that she was a leading figure in the popularisation of machine-independent programming languages – for the non-technical, this means the ability to write a computer programme using a structure that is somewhat understandable on sight by humans, rather than what the first computers used, which was a basic 'machine code' that was incredibly hard for anyone looking at it to comprehend. Hopper's important groundwork eventually went on to be developed into the programming language called COBOL, a language still used in computer systems today. In contrast to many whose contributions to the early development of computers was hushed up because of the need for secrecy in times of war,

Commodore Grace M. Hopper

Grace Hopper's work is comparatively well recognised and not only is the *National Energy Research Scientific Computing Center*'s supercomputer named 'Hopper' in her memory, but also – as she was a high-ranking officer in the United States Navy – an Arleigh Burke class guided-missile destroyer is named *USS Hopper* in her honour.

Hedy Lamarr
(1914–2000)

Few people could have had as interesting a career as Hedy Lamarr. The earliest days of her adult life saw her feature in a controversial 1933 German movie called *Ecstasy* – considered by some film historians as the first non-pornographic film to feature depictions of sexual intercourse. Not long after this however, she fled Nazi Germany for Paris where she met Louis B. Mayer (of MGM fame) who offered her a Hollywood contract. From the 1930s through to the 1950s, Lamarr was an extremely well-loved actress, starring in a number of both popular and critically-acclaimed films. However her larger contribution to humankind actually came from work she undertook with a composer named George Antheil. Together the two developed a radio guidance system designed to be used by torpedoes. The genius of the system was that it used a variety of techniques (such as frequency hopping) to overcome the problem of enemy jamming countermeasures. Although the technology made no difference to the Second World War (being so advanced that the US Navy did not begin to use it for its intended purpose until the 1960s!) it has an impact on almost everything we do today – Bluetooth, GPS and Wi-Fi all *directly* benefit from the system Lamarr invented. For someone with such a massive influence on today's modern technology, Hedy Lamarr is relatively unknown; she was however inducted into the *National Inventors Hall of Fame* in 2014 and recently a number of documentaries by the likes of *The Discovery Channel* and others have begun to tell of her incredible invention to a wider audience.

Hedy Lamarr in 1940

RACHEL CARSON
(1907–1964)

Rachel Carson had already written a successful trilogy of books when in the late 1950s she became more and more interested in conservation. One of her key interests was the effect of synthetic pesticides, which she believed were causing a number of environmental issues which were not being addressed by governments and other scientists of the day. Her 1962 book *Silent Spring* managed to bring these issues to the attention of the general public, and its lasting legacy was the nationwide ban on DDT (amongst other harmful pesticides) which caused environmental damage on such a scale that only today, some fifty years later, are we seeing its reversal. Since the awareness brought by Carson's book, focus on environmental issues has increased greatly; as a direct result, the *US Environmental Protection Agency* was created which has been influential in protecting the environment from a wide range of threats. After she died as a result of being weakened by treatment for breast cancer, Carson was given the prestigious honour of the *Presidential Medal of Freedom* for her work in raising awareness of the need to protect our environment.

HENRIETTA LACKS
(1920–1951)

Henrietta's contribution to science is not *strictly* one that is deliberate. This does not however mean that it is any less important that others – in fact, it raised some of the most important questions ever posed regarding medical ethics and the right of an individual to their own biological material. In 1951, Henrietta was taken to Johns Hopkins Hospital after suffering from severe abdominal pain and abnormal bleeding in the area. She was diagnosed with cervical cancer, and although she was given chemotherapy, she died in October the same year. Prior to her death however,

Rachel Carson

doctors had removed two cervical samples from her body without her knowledge or consent. The cells that had been removed were amongst others that were provided to Dr George Gey, who was conducting cell research. He noticed an unusual quality in Henrietta's cells; whilst most normal cells which survived just a few days, hers appeared much more durable. Gey isolated and then multiplied one of her cells, creating a cell line which he called *HeLa* (from the first two letters of her first and last names). The creation of this cell line completely revolutionised medical research; the HeLa line was used to develop a vaccine for polio, and over the last five decades more than ten thousand patents involving the HeLa line have been registered; the cells are used for may medical experiments, from studying diseases to testing new products and treatments. Whilst it is true that many lives have surely been saved because of the HeLa cell line, the questionable way in which they were procured raises many questions of ethics. The American government has essentially ruled that companies can commercially profit from Lacks' cells without needing to pay any financial compensation to her estate, and her family were not even consulted when a strain of HeLa cells had their genome published. On a positive note, Henrietta Lacks was granted a posthumous honorary degree, and she has been honoured at the Smithsonian Institute.

Rosalind Franklin
(1920–1958)

Whilst many people credit James Watson and Francis Crick with the discovery of the structure of DNA, the story isn't quite that simple. In fact, Rosalind Franklin's contribution is so important that many feel that she deserves as much of the limelight – and perhaps even more so – than her more famous counterparts. Whilst earning her Ph.D. in physical chemistry at Cambridge University, Franklin learned two techniques in particular that she applied to

DNA fibres – crystallography and X-ray diffraction. It was these techniques that allowed her to actually photograph the structure of DNA, and without these images, Crick and Watson would almost certainly not have been able to support their proposed model of DNA. One photograph in particular ('photograph 51') is considered to be critical evidence in identifying the structure of DNA; Franklin herself actually refined an X-ray machine which allowed over one hundred hours of exposure in order to take the photograph. Despite her huge contribution to the foundation of modern genetic biology, the only reference to Rosalind's months of research was one single footnote in Watson and Crick's thesis. Today, it is widely recognised that a huge amount of their work would have been impossible without Franklin's contribution, and the *true* history of the discovery of the structure of DNA is slowly beginning to become more widely acknowledged.

Chapter Ten
Business

Coco Chanel
(1883–1971)

Until the First World War, women's clothing had traditionally been restrictive and impractical. Coco Chanel helped change this by making it simpler and more suited to everyday living. She was the first designer to introduce trousers and suits for women, and pioneered items of clothing such as the collarless cardigan jacket and the floating evening scarf. Chanel was a controversial figure; she closed her shops during the Second World War, stating that it was 'not a time for fashion' – although the true reason was likely to include retaliation against the workers she employed, who had been demanding better conditions! Her legacy is that women today can dress for themselves, and not for the pleasure of men.

Mary Quant
(1934–)

Although the truth about miniskirts is that their popularity in the swinging sixties was the result of a number of different factors, every movement has a figurehead – and so, Mary Quant is considered the most instrumental figure in bringing the decade's defining piece of clothing to the attention of the fashionable youth. Her contribution to fashion – and in fact society as a whole – is actually much more than that however. Quant encouraged young people to dress in clothes that were designed for their own pleasure, rather than to please others. In doing this, she brought the masses to fashion, rather than the other way round. In fashion circles, Mary Quant is considered one of the three most influential figures, alongside Coco Chanel and Christian Dior. When talking about how the miniskirt came about, Quant credited its invention to 'the girls on the King's Road' – she described how she was simply making clothes in which one could move, jump about or run for the bus; the customers would ask for the fit to

Coco Chanel in 1970

Elizabeth Arden in 1939

be shorter and shorter. It *is* generally accepted that she gave the miniskirt its name – it borrowed 'mini' from her favourite make of car, another icon of 60s Britain. Mary Quant's contributions are well recognised, and in 1966 she was awarded the OBE, being 'upgraded' to a Dame in 2015.

Elizabeth Arden
(1878–1966)

At the peak of her success, Elizabeth Arden was one of the wealthiest women on the planet. Her 'real' name was actually Florence Nightingale Graham, although she went by her better-known alternative from very early on in her career – the word 'Arden' in fact came from the name of a local farm! After studying beauty techniques in the high-class salons of Paris, Arden created a number of her own cosmetics and began to open up her own beauty establishments across America. Essentially, Elizabeth Arden changed the entire nature of the cosmetics industry. Before the popularity of her beauty products, make-up was generally considered to be something worn only by prostitutes and the lower classes. Through appealing to middle-aged women who desired a more youthful appearance and the provision of high quality products in an upmarket setting, Arden changed this, and within a decade or two of her business expansion, women across the world were applying beauty products on a daily basis. Whilst some would argue that the creation of such an industry is a double-edged sword at best, Arden certainly offered women the ability to choose their own looks, and for her contribution to the world she was given the *Legion d'Honneur* by the French Government in 1962.

Katharine Graham
(1917-2001)

The lack of equality in business is most apparent at boardroom level, with the vast majority of not only CEOs but even simply boardroom members being male. Katharine Graham is notable therefore not just for her success in business, but also in being the first female CEO of a *Fortune 500* company, which she achieved in 1972. By that point, Graham had effectively been in charge of *The Washington Post* for almost ten years. In 1963 she had taken over from her husband who had suffered from mental health issues; he tragically committed suicide after being admitted to a psychiatric hospital. The business had in fact been Katharine's father's, although she always insisted it had never bothered her that it had been handed down to her husband rather than from father to daughter. Katharine's leadership was strong, in fact seeing the paper through the most successful and influential period in its history. During her tenure, the paper oversaw the reporting of the *Watergate* scandal which eventually brought down the Nixon government. Katharine Graham showed that the gender of a company's leader made no difference to how well it could be run, a lesson that seems still not been fully learned today. She proved to be one of journalism's most influential figures of the 20th century and her 1997 memoirs received the Pulitzer Prize.

Dame Anita Roddick
(1942-2007)

Few people have had such a major impact on consumer ethics as that brought about by Anita Roddick. In 1976 she opened a store called *The Body Shop* which aimed to offer women high quality skin care products which were marketed with 'truth rather than hype'. The key concept behind the store was that the products were natural, free from ingredients tested on animals, and were environmentally friendly. Launched at a time when awareness of the need to look after our planet was increasing, Roddick once described the success of the original store as a 'series of brilliant accidents', coming along at the right time for a wave of ethically-conscious consumers who not only wanted to feel morally sound about the products they bought, but could afford them too. As the business's success increased and more stores opened, Roddick never sacrificed the principles on which the brand was founded. Famously, The Body Shop was one of the first major businesses to promote fair trade with third world countries, at a time when many companies grew rich on the basis of paying minimal amounts for goods sourced from the developing world. Whilst always keeping a close eye on her business, Roddick also was an active campaigner for a range of issues, notably speaking on behalf of *Greenpeace* and being deeply involved with *The Big Issue*, a magazine project designed to assist the homeless. When asked for an example of an ethical business leader, Dame Anita Roddick is still today one of the first names usually mentioned, and her influence can still be seen in the increasing standards the cosmetics industry has subscribed to over the last four decades, having learned that many consumers buy with a conscience.

Chapter Eleven

Media & Entertainment

Lois Weber
(1879-1939)

Hollywood may be prone to a little exaggeration, however when it comes to Lois Weber, it is certainly not over the top to consider her as the 'most important female director the American film industry has known' – as she has previously been dubbed. Weber is considered one of the most important and influential directors in the silent film era, and can be said to have been the industry's first true *auteur*. Although she brought between two and four hundred films to the screen, sadly less than twenty have been fully preserved, and little is known about many of them. Her films were important for both artistic and technical reasons. On the one hand, their subject matter raised the kind of questions about human nature and society that the best movies still address today; on the other, she pioneered certain techniques – perhaps the best known being the 'split screen' method that she used in her 1913 release *Suspense*. In the silent era she did even experiment with sound, using various techniques to sync audio with pictures. Some of her developments were controversial; in 1915 Weber's film *Hypocrites* brought her to the attention of the censors, as it was the first Hollywood film to feature full-frontal nudity. She was also the subject of discussion a year later when *Where Are My Children?* brought the issues of abortion and birth control to the public consciousness. Weber's achievements are well recognised even though she is no longer a household name; her star on the *Hollywood Walk of Fame* is of course the 'ultimate' accolade for those in her profession.

Katherine Hepburn
(1907–2003)

The traditional Hollywood golden age leading lady was blonde and subservient. Not so Katherine Hepburn! She showed that one could be a successful actress whilst retaining independence

Lois Weber, date unknown

and always did things her own way. Even since school Hepburn had been rather rebellious, once suspended for smoking; later in life she admitting to enjoying the occasional skinny-dip in the middle of the night! Katherine still today holds the record for the most number of Oscars won for *Best Actress* (four) despite her reputation for being a 'difficult' actress to work with – until later life she was almost always reluctant to give interviews to the press. Katherine Hepburn's life is perhaps best summed up by her own words: *"If you obey all the rules, you miss all the fun".*

DOLLY PARTON
(1946-)

The 'First Lady' of country music, Dolly Parton has been performing professionally since she was just ten years old. Having grown up in a poor neighbourhood (and being one of twelve children) her family did not have much; she did however get great pleasure from singing in church. When a relative noticed her musical talent, he gave Dolly her first guitar, and she quickly moved on from singing other people's songs to writing her own. Whilst at school she studied hard, but put plenty of time into writing and performing – even as a teenager she was a regular fixture on local radio and TV stations. After graduating she moved to Nashville – the home of country music – to develop her career further. In the late 1960s Dolly began to grow into a nationwide sensation; her incredible voice, beautiful songs and warm personality endeared her to all those watching, and within a few years she was known across the world. Dolly is one of the few artists to straddle both the country music genre and general 'pop' music, having had a number of hits in the pop music charts as well as dominating the specialist country music genre ones. In the 1980s she branched out into other areas, most notably acting (with her hit comedy *9 to 5* perhaps being her best known work) and famously a theme park, *Dollywood*, which remains to this day one of Tennessee's top tourist attractions.

Oprah Winfrey
(1954–)

One of America's most influential media figures, Oprah was the first woman to have her own talk show. She is known for promoting a range of liberal causes, and has used her talk show to break down barriers on many issues, from those affecting gay and lesbian men and women to those specifically faced by women, the black community and many others. With a huge following, Oprah has always tried to use her influence to change the world for the better, and is credited with changing the very nature of television, bringing to the screen a much more personal and intimate form of communication. One study suggested that Oprah's TV show had more influence than any other when it came to the integration of LGBT people into the mainstream. In 2004 she became America's first (and at the time of writing, *only*) black female billionaire. Winfrey is considered to be one of history's great philanthropists and in 2013 Barack Obama (whose campaign for presidency she had supported) awarded her the *Presidential Medal of Freedom*.

Emma Watson
(1990-)

Many people know Emma Watson as the actress who played Hermione in the *Harry Potter* films; she could therefore be included in this book purely for the pleasure she has given to millions of fans across the globe. However, it is actually due to her work for human rights that she is featured here. Much of Emma's activism comes from her role as a UN 'Goodwill Ambassador', and she personally launched the campaign *HeForShe* which focuses on gender equality. Emma has toured the world in her fight to improve the treatment of women and has spoken out against gender-based assumptions, media sexualisation and threatening behaviour. Watson herself has been the subject of much unwarranted hateful communication, often from elements of the population who fail to understand her call for equality and the rights of women. She has worked hard to educate people about the concepts of feminism, and right the perception of 'man-hating' that some have of the feminist movement – incredibly she actually received threatening communications just hours after making one speech that addressed these issues; Watson went on record as saying that such acts just made her even more determined to continue her work! She has contributed to campaigns that aim to promote education for girls in areas of the world where that is not the norm, and has also called for more women to participate in politics. It seems that her work is beginning to make a difference, as at the time of writing, Emma Watson is named as the 25th most influential person in the world.

And Finally...

Queen Victoria
(1819–1901)

Victoria never expected to ascend to the throne; it was only because of three of her uncles' untimely deaths in succession that she became monarch at a time of massive change. Perhaps because she had never expected to rule, Victoria had a very different personality to many other leaders, but it was her very nature which saw Britain lead the world during her reign. The achievements of Victoria and her country are, of course, well documented elsewhere and this book could easily be twice as long if just a few of them were included! Suffice to say that Victoria oversaw industrial change on an epic scale, society develop into something almost completely unrecognisable between the time of her coronation and her later years, the enormous expansion of the British Empire (on which, it was said, the sun never set) – and yet remained perhaps the most well-loved monarch the country had ever seen. Although her marriage to Prince Albert (in fact her first cousin) was effectively an arranged one, the two fell very much in love and when Albert died prematurely, Victoria essentially spent the rest of her life in mourning. Contrary to the way she is thought of today, for much of her life Victoria was a vibrant, joyful figure, active if not athletic in her youth. Her nine children married into various noble families on the continent, meaning that in her latter years she was known as *the grandmother of Europe*. With the exception of Queen Elizabeth II, Victoria's reign was the longest of any British monarch, and it is unlikely any other leader will see the kind of change that she did during her time on the throne.

1882 Photograph of Queen Victoria

Printed in Dunstable, United Kingdom